FROM SIL TO STO

The Power of Sharing your Story

By

Jumoke Akintunde

Thank you!!

FROM SILENCE TO STORY:
The Power of Sharing your Story

©2024 Jumoke Akintunde
ISBN: 9798343002584

All rights reserved. No part of this publication may be reproduced, distributed, or transmitted in any form or by any means, including photocopying, recording, or other electronic or mechanical methods, without the prior written permission of the publisher, except in the case of brief quotations embodied in critical reviews and certain other non-commercial uses permitted by copyright law.

Design by Golden Truth Publishing
Berwick, NS, Canada.
www.goldentruth.pro
&
Jumoke Akintunde
England, UK
www.jumokeakintunde.com

Contents

Foreword	9
Acknowledgements	10
Dedication	11
Chapter 1 Reveal It: You Have The Message To The World	12
Why This Book?	20
Who Is The Book For?	24
What To Expect	25
Call To Action	27
Chapter 2 Your Unique Story: How to Identify, Embrace, and Share It	29
Your Story	30
Types Of Stories	34
What Is Your Story?	37
Visual Representation of How to Establish Your Story	41
Call To Action	43
Chapter 3 Your Narrative, Your Strength: The Power of Personal Stories	45
Who Tells The Story Better?	46
Top Reasons Why You Need To Share Your Story?	50
How To Share Your Story	58
Comparisons between Biography, Autobiography and Memoir	62
Examples of True-life Story Drama	70
Ways To Share Your Story	72
Your Experience	74
Call To Action:	76
Chapter 4 From Struggle to Strength: My Path of Faith and Resilience	77
My Story: Nuggets	78

Before 'I do' Nuggets	81
After 'I do' and Still Doing Nuggets	85
A Twist	89
The UK Systems	94
My Circle	97
Call To Action	102

Chapter 5
Unseen Battles: Turning Pain into Power — 104

What You Can Share: Your Pains	105
Role Models Of Pain	108
Process Of Pain	112
Top 10 Positives Of Pain	114
Identifying Your Pain	117
Guide To Identifying The Pain Points In Your Life	117
Acceptance Of The Pain	124
The Pain Acceptance Jigsaw	125
Call To Action	126

Chapter 6
Persevere to Triumph: Becoming the Next Success Story — 128

It Is Not The End Of The Story	129
Top Success Stories	134
Why Some Succeed And Some Struggle	143
The Growth Mind-set Table	146
Lyrics:	151
Call to Action	153

Chapter 7
Celebrate and Share: The Power of Your Victories — 154

What You Can Share: Your Victories	155
Discover The Positives Of Victories	156
Mistakes To Avoid In Wins	158
Call to Action	163

Chapter 8
My Story: Trusting God's Timing — 164

    The God Factor — 165
    Why Does God Allow Pain? — 167
    Does God Answer Prayers? — 171
    Waiting: Why Answers To Prayers Are Delayed — 179
    When It All Does Not Seem To Make Sense — 185
    I Will Sing — 186
    Call to Action — 191

Chapter 9
My Story: Wins And Pains — 192

    My Wins — 193
    Your Wins — 193
    Salvation — 194
    Career — 195
    Relocation — 198
    Relocating To The UK — 199
    Relocating Within UK — 199
    My Pains: My Griefs — 201
    Positives of Grief — 204
    Negatives of grief: Mistakes you want to avoid — 209
    Gossip — 215
    Betrayals — 221
    Top 15 Nuggets — 225
    Call To Action — 232

Appendix — 233

    Quotes — 233
    Sources — 254

You will encounter bullying in life. The bully could be a medical condition, a person, or something else entirely. Whether you are a victim or a winner in this situation depends on how you respond to it. With the help of real-world experiences from this book, "From Silence to Story: The Power of Sharing Your Story," you will learn how to deal with life's bullies, get stronger, and become a role model for others who may have felt hopeless.

Jumoke has written a uniquely captivating work that promises to heal the silent sufferers across all boundaries and give them a voice.

Titilayo Omotayo Alade
Author "What Do You Have?
Contemporary Success Strategies
from an Ancient Story"

I agree with Jumoke: You are the best person to share your version of your story. Your story is exclusive, powerful, and important; even more, it makes you important.

This book will inspire you to share your story. It will show you that one of the most powerful things you can do is to write your own story.

Godman Akinlabi
Global Lead Pastor
The Elevation Church
Lagos, Nigeria

In this book, Jumoke explores the profound importance of storytelling, as emphasised by Emily Dickinson's analogy of life as a journey. She highlights and reinforces how sharing our experiences can transform us and connect us to culture and humanity. Jumoke demonstrates the multi-dimensional nature of storytelling and its impact on personal and societal growth. As a book writing coach and author, I strongly recommend this book for those seeking to embrace the power of their own narrative, underscoring that our stories are invaluable gifts that inspire, educate, and connect us.

David Adabale
Purpose & Business Coach/ Author

Foreword

It was Chinua Achebe who said, *"If you don't like someone's story, write your own."* Your story is as unique as your fingerprint, and it is worth sharing.

This book will inspire you to share your story. It will show you that one of the most powerful things you can do is to write your own story.

In digesting the gems embedded in this book, look out for Chapter 5. It will trigger and ignite something you have kept buried for so long. That mess can become a message!

If we share stories of only our trophies and triumphs without our failures and flaws, we will give people the false impression that you can win a war without engaging in a battle; that you can be a star without scars, have a crown without a cross; that you can win championship without hardship. Share not just your success stories but also your pains, flaws, and falls.

I agree with Jumoke: *You are the best person to share your version of your story. Your story is exclusive, powerful, and important; even more, it makes you important.*

Godman Akinlabi
Global Lead Pastor
The Elevation Church

Acknowledgements

This book has lingered in my thoughts for a considerable time, and I am grateful to God Almighty for it now being in your hands. I have a lot of people to appreciate for being part of my journey; without them, my story has no depth.

I want to specially thank my husband, Adewale, who has been a constant source of inspiration. Thank you for all you do. I also want to appreciate my children; your unwavering support and understanding have been amazing. Thank you all for standing by me throughout the process of writing this book.

I want to express my gratitude to my parents and siblings. I did not get to choose the family I was born into; however, I am immensely grateful for the choice God made for me.

I would like to specially appreciate my editing team - Ololade Akintunde, Mr Olukayode, Mrs Yetunde Olusanya, Mrs Ope Orekoya, Oyinkansola Akintunde and Mrs Titilayo Alade. Thank you all for your invaluable contributions.

A huge thank you to Pastor David Adabale, for your assistance that was instrumental to the making of this book. I am grateful for your guidance.

Dedication

To the blessed memory of my dad, whose love, wisdom, and guidance continue to inspire me every day. This book is a tribute to your enduring legacy.

This book is dedicated to YOU.

You have a story, and it is unique. You have an incomparable story, and it is the focus of this book. You deserve a special treat. Your narrative is eagerly anticipated, being read, viewed, and listened to by the world.

Share your story!
Make it clear!
Let the tale of you unfold!
Unleash your story!
The world awaits your story.

CHAPTER 1

Reveal It: You Have the Message To The World

CHAPTER HIGHLIGHTS:

- You have a story, let this book inspire you to share your story.
- Share your story.
- Your story is a service to mankind, serve it.
- Your life is a tale of many stories, starting from the moment you were born to your current position and circumstances.
- The world has a place for you.

Life is a highway! Life is a journey!

The journey of your life is brimming with stories, from cradle till present. This book encompasses some selection from my stories - The tale of a woman helped by God. I am not perfect; I am a work-in-progress (WIP), complete with strengths and weaknesses.

Life has been a lengthy voyage, and I am still on the journey, encountering discoveries, pains, challenges, and celebrations. This is to tell you that the journey of life is as important as the destination. Let me start with one of my many stories to buttress the above point.

I used to believe that travelling by plane, whether in first class, business class or economy was all the same — we would all get to the destination at the same time. That perception changed when my husband and brother encouraged me to try the first class. On various occasions, my husband and I experienced it and honestly, it was exclusive. Prior to boarding at the VIP lounge, we enjoyed exotic food and drinks and before others completed boarding, drinks were served numerously. I was frequently asked how they could assist me, with various offers and options, the experience was truly elite. On another trip to the same destination, I flew economy, and there was a noticeable difference in the experience. Service was provided along with everyone else, no elite treatment. Despite heading to the same destination, the experiences were different, each with its own story to tell. It became clear that the journey itself is as important as reaching the destination.

Emily Dickinson, in her poem, *Because I Could Not Stop for Death*, compared life to a journey complete with a carriage ride.

Your life is about the journey, not the destination. Irrespective of what you are working towards, it is crucial to take a few moments to appreciate the present and share your story. When you share your story, it allows you to pause and reflect. You have travelled a long way to get here.

Everyone has a story that is worth sharing. You have a story that needs to be heard. You need to share that story, particularly when you share it with love, compassion, clarity, and authenticity.

> *"Our stories are powerful, especially when they are fuelled with love, compassion, courage, and the strong desire to help those who are just beginning their healing journey. Stories are powerful, so please consider sharing your story. Your story, your voice, and your message matters."*
>
> **Treena Wynes**

Over the years, I have been open to and comfortable with sharing stories within the public domain. In fact, you would find them on several social media platforms such as — birthday celebrations, wedding anniversaries, educational and professional qualifications. However, I was not really sharing my challenges, mistakes, pains; looking back, it seems like I kept these aspects compartmentalised. I considered them to be my personal stories, a private space not meant for intrusion. In this book, I am stepping beyond that boundary, sharing not only my wins but also my pains. I want you to understand my background, my perspectives, and possibly learn from my story to cultivate self-love. In the process of sharing my story comes reflections and expressions of gratitude.

I am privileged to be the author of this book, sharing my personal journey with the intention of empowering you to tell your own story. In my role as a leader and counsellor, I have had the privilege of supporting others listening to their private stories. Therefore, as I embark on this writing journey, I extend my appreciation to those who have entrusted me with their stories. I recognise the courage it takes to share, even in confidence. For me, putting my story out there, is a daunting experience, as it makes me feel vulnerable to lay bare my private experiences in public. I am not ignorant of the fact that vulnerability can lead to amazing connections, miracles, healing, compassion, and impactful changes, all making the world a better place for everyone. This is humanity, a deep human experience. And sharing some of my personal stories is my way of acknowledging that recovery comes from a form of healing that brings closure — something we all need for every heartache.

I do not want you to be silent about your story, I am not going to be. Do not deny any parts of your story, neither suppress nor silence the voice of your pains and your past, as your story is your strength. Your story is powerful and matters, there is power in telling your story.

As a Christian, how does the following scripture relate to you?

> *Therefore, if anyone is in Christ, he is a new creation; old things have passed away; behold, all things have become new.*
>
> **2 Corinthians 5:17**

"Your story makes you special, all your experiences, your pains, your wins; it makes you and makes your story."

Not denying your past, sharing your pains, challenges, hurts etc? This can only reassure you that you can have a fresh start, no matter the past pains. The above bible verse talks about the new birth; The beauty that God has made from your ashes. The ashes that should not stall you from sharing your story. Jesus said, if the pain becomes so intense that you feel you can never move on or forgive a person, you must forgive; let go and move on. This is freedom, liberation. Remember, Jesus spoke in parables, He told loads of stories. You need to share yours.

> *"Life is a song; we each get to write our own lyrics."*

I want you to picture several aspects of your life, this picture is a visual fiction or non-fiction of your life that needs to be told as a story. Metaphorically, life is said to be many things:

"Life is a puzzle; you can only see the picture when you put all the pieces together."

"Your life story is a gift and should be treated as such."

Emily V. Gordon

"The universe is made of stories, not atoms."

Muriel Rukeyser.

Numerous stories have had a profound impact on your life and our world, from political, social, to personal resonance. Works such as Chinua Achebe's Things Fall Apart, Mary Shelley's Frankenstein, Homer's The Odyssey, along with countless stories presented as parables in the bible, continue to resonate with and influence you.

In The Narrative Complexity of Ordinary Life: Tales from the Coffee Shop by William L. Randall, he mentioned the four levels within which the concept of "a life story" can be understood—the level of existence (outside story), experience (inside story), expression (inside-out story), and impression (outside-in story).

In this book, I will be discussing the importance of a story (your story). How sharing your story is a part of humanity. Your story is humane. How your story helps to preserve posterity, your culture, your values, connect to the world and the universal truth. How your story comprises your experiences, the twists, the turns, the challenges, the pains, wins; all these makes you. It is the whole essence of you. You are your story, and it makes you special.

Discussing your narrative and openly sharing it, serves to teach your values. It allows people to know what your challenges have been, understand your journey and celebrate your wins. It is important to celebrate success and scars. Your narrative is designed to appeal to senses and emotions which is why you need to give your story a voice. By doing so, it can evoke other people's emotions, enabling them to learn from your experiences. Sharing your journey not only draws the attention of a broader audience easily, but also has the potential to make a significant impact on peoples' lives.

When you share your story, you foster creative thinking, it helps to build your emotional intelligence and others, it builds your confidence, and you can tell the world of all that you have gone through. By sharing your story, you have the opportunity to reflect and appreciate. You reflect on the experiences you have been through (the past), appreciate and understand what you are currently going through (the present) and propel yourself forward (future). This process not only allows for self-reflection but also fosters the journey of life.

Sharing your story declares the glory and wonderful works of God to the nations of the earth, passing survival, inheritance, and continuity to generations. Psalm 96:3: "Declare his glory among the nations, his marvellous works among all the peoples!"

WHY THIS BOOK?

Authoring this book took a long time. I drafted a few manuscripts, and daily asked myself, why a new book, why this book? Until I came to the realisation that my story, your story, and everyone's story is powerfully unique and need to be shared. This book makes me feel fulfilled.

I thought I should write and share my story to impact and connect with and influence my world. If this book is making a difference in just your life, I am fulfilled. Martin Luther King Jr. said, "Never underestimate the difference YOU can make in the lives of others." I know, with immense joy, that this book will influence your life and gradually take over the world. And I also know, you will pay it forward.

"If you can't pay it back, pay it forward."

Catherine Ryan Hyde

This book holds deep personal significance for me, as a lot of the stories I shared, have played a crucial role in shaping me into the woman I am today. Books, in particular, have changed my life and perspective on various issues and topics. I strongly believe that this book will positively impact and change your life as well. Quoting Mike Anderson, "We need to know that we make a positive difference through the work we do." This book answers my own yearnings and questions, such as, 'How can I reach my world?', 'How can I give back to others?', 'What value can I add to your life?', 'What efforts can I engage in with others?', 'Why I do what I do?'. Through this book, I aim to help to unleash the stories and potentials of many.

Writing this book gives me a sense of serving and giving to humanity. Muhammad Ali said, *"Service to others is the rent you pay for your room here on earth."*

This is my way of giving to you. Give, and it will be given to you: good measure, pressed down, shaken together, and running over will be put into your bosom. For with the same measure that you use, it will be measured back to you.

Luke 6:38.

A great man, Ron Kenoly, once sang a song, titled Give to the Lord. And I love the song. See part of the lyrics below:

Give and it will come back to

you. Good measure, pressed

down, shaken together, and

running over. Give and it will

come back to you.

When you give, "you" give to the Lord.

Also, I once read and heard quotes by Myles Munroe and Les Brown.

> *"The graveyard is the richest place on the surface of the earth because there you will see the books that were not published, ideas that were not harnessed, songs that were not sung, and drama pieces that were never acted."*
>
> **Myles Munroe**

> *"The graveyard is the richest place on earth, because it is here that you will find all the hopes and dreams that were never fulfilled, the books that were never written, the songs that were never sung, the inventions that were never shared, the cures that were never discovered, all because someone was too afraid to take that first step, keep with the problem, or determined to carry out their dream."*
>
> **Les Brown**

This kept playing in my mind, several times, over the years and I thought why would I take the books in me to the graveyard, why rob the world of my story? I should not and neither should you. I desire that I die empty, writing all the books, fulfilling all my dreams. I love sharing, so why keep my story to myself and you keep yours to yourself.

> *I tell you the truth, unless a kernel of wheat is planted in the soil and dies, it remains alone. But its death will produce many new kernels—a plentiful harvest of new lives.*
>
> **John 12:24 NLT.**

There is a man that had some life stories to share, he kept procrastinating, promising to share the story. Unfortunately, he died. He had life's important lessons, but he never got to sharing them. Never take those peculiar, important stories, songs, and hymns to the graveyard. Death has no use for these tales.

I am thrilled to see this book in your hands. Throughout the years, I have harboured numerous ideas for books, many of which remain confined to my thoughts. I drafted a few; but the persistent question of 'why another book?' held me back from publishing. The good news is that I finally have compelling answers to that question, motivating me to bring this book into the world. I am glad it is a dream come true.

WHO IS THE BOOK FOR?

This book is for everyone, including you. It emphasises the need to share your story, underscoring that your narrative matters. Your story has the potential to inspire, encourage, challenge, and empower others. But how can others hear or read your story if you do not share it? I have chosen to share snippets of some of my stories – both victories and challenges.

This book is for Christians and non-Christians, to enable you to tell your story and, subsequently, impact your life and others positively. Concisely, this book is for everyone, particularly churches, faith institutions, young at heart, and vulnerable groups.

As imperative as this book encourages the sharing of your story, in addition, I would like to encourage you to share this book (my story) with others. Recommend it, review it, talk about it, make it a reference book. Thank you!

To that girl, woman the world is full of opportunities waiting for you to explore and challenges to overcome. Remember, you are strong, tough, capable, and deserving of every dream you hold in your heart. Education (formal or informal) is a power you can deploy, and with it, you can achieve anything you set your mind to. Jesus Christ is a great enabling power, which can help you do all things. Don't let anyone or anything limit your potential. Embrace your uniqueness, believe in yourself, and never be afraid to dare, to stand up and shine. The future is yours to create, and I believe in you every step of the way. No holds barred. Keep pushing forward because you are unstoppable! Great power lies in you! You can! Go girl!

WHAT TO EXPECT

This book will explore the significance of telling your story, its benefits, the challenges you may have faced, the triumphs it may yield. Through this book, I will be sharing my personal story with you, providing a first-hand account of my experiences. This book focuses on why you need to tell your story, guides you on how to share it, and emphasises the power it holds.

Chapter 1

The purpose of this book is to encourage and challenge you, inspiring not only you but also others to share their stories and make a difference in someone's world. The positive outcomes are bound to make a meaningful impact on both your personal and professional life. Join me on this journey to really discover why sharing your story can have a positive impact on someone's life. There is no tale, no honour in concealing your story. There is a story, hidden, within every achievement.

> *"No story, no glory."*

There is no tale, no honour in concealing your story. There is a story, hidden, within every achievement.

No story, no glory. Behind every glory is a story. Everyone shining around you has a story. Unleash yours!

Stay tuned, reading this book and appreciate the invaluable reasons for sharing your story and subsequently sharing this book with others through recommendations, reviews, or referrals.

CALL TO ACTION

▶ **Identify Your Story:** What personal story, unique recipe, innovative idea or inspiring book do you have to share? Reflect and select a narrative that resonates deeply with you.

▶ **Overcome Hesitations:** Consider any barriers that are preventing you from sharing your story. Is it fear, lack of resources, or uncertainty about its reception? Acknowledge these challenges so you can address them.

▶ **Define Your Audience:** Who needs to hear your story? Identifying your target audience will help tailor your narrative to engage and inspire the right listeners or readers effectively.

▶ **Choose Your Sharing Method:** How do you want your story to be conveyed? Options might include writing a blog post, creating a video, publishing a book, or giving a
speech. Decide on the format that best suits your message and skills.

▶ **What support does your Story need:** Which team do you need to work with? How do you get them and share the story. Would the support team be free, paid for, make the enquiries, and get started.

▶ **Select Your Platform:** Where is the best place to share your story? Choose a platform that aligns with your audience and content type, whether it's social media, a personal blog, a community event, or elsewhere.

CHAPTER 2

Your Unique Story: How to Identify, Embrace, and Share It

CHAPTER HIGHLIGHTS

- Identify and establish your story.
- Never deny any part of your story.
- What is your story? You have a story.
- Your story can be shared in different ways.
- Identify your audience, to effectively deliver your story.

YOUR STORY

In this chapter, the focal point will be the exploration of what a story is, addressing the question, "what is your Story?" The content will include tips to identify your unique story, diverse types of stories and how you can effectively share your story.

Story is known to be a chronology, anecdote, plot, tale, article, narrative, account, history of various incidents and or events in one's life. This could be your statement, narrative, account, and a version of your journey on this earth, at a phase. Anecdote - a brief account of something that happened to you; this may be remarkable or ordinary. This type of story would be the major viewpoint of this book, your personal story. I am going to be sharing my stories and I believe you will certainly get a lot of nuggets from my life story.

During my formative years, stories played a significant role in shaping my understanding of life. My late grandmother, of blessed memory, enriched my childhood with tales about the tortoise and lion, as well as bible stories and accounts of her hometown, genealogy, family life. Most of these stories had lessons, and would prompt questions from my grandmother, questions like, "What did you learn?" and "What is the lesson from the story?" My parents, continuing this tradition, would also gather us together, especially during power outages by the then National Electric Power Authority (NEPA), Electric

Supplier in Nigeria, now Power Holding Company of Nigeria (PHCN). They shared stories of their growing up: the neighbourhood, siblings, and the challenges they faced. We prayed together, and witnessed the answers to those prayers, affirming my childhood belief in the existence of a God in heaven. Additionally, my siblings would share their boarding school experiences, as we all went to boarding schools. I have carried on this practice with my children, though with caution, to avoid sharing stories that of people that have caused me hurt. Children tend to never forget those who hurt their precious ones, even when the parents have moved on.

As a child, growing up, I encountered a prevailing belief in the community, that favoured boys over girls. Despite the nurturing and support from my immediate family, societal bias was still at play. There were various stereotypes such as, 'a girl's future is the kitchen,' 'gender inequality', 'child marriage'. Interestingly, on a particular occasion, a self-proclaimed prophet predicted that I would not complete my education and would become a teenage parent. This prophecy offended me deeply, prompting me to confront and dismiss the so-called prophet. I knew what I wanted and immediately refused this bleak prediction. This perceived misconception fuelled my resolve to challenge and correct the damaging perspective surrounding the girl child. I made up my mind, as a young girl, to commit myself to dispelling the misconceptions associated with being a girl child: 'A girl child is not worthy of education', 'she will get pregnant in the course of educating her', 'a boy child is better than a girl child' and so on.

> *"Many stories matter. Stories have been used to dispossess and to malign. But stories can also be used to empower, and to humanise. Stories can break the dignity of a people. But stories can also repair that broken dignity."*
>
> ### ***Chimamanda Ngozi Adichie***

> *"Whether you know it or not, your desire to write comes from the urge to not just be "creative," it is a need (one every human being on earth has) to help others. A well-told story is a gift to the reader, listener, and viewer because it teaches them how to confront their own discomforts."*
>
> ### ***Shawn Coyne***

Great power lies with a story, when you write a story or tell a story, it helps people connect, empowers, build people, and even build you. As such, there is humongous power in your story and sharing it.

So, you can see through and appreciate my world, and the world can see through you, by sharing of my story, your story, our stories.

I am glad to say that as a woman, I continue to be the author of my life story, reshaping it with the several chapters that challenge and correct prevailing biases. A testament to the truth that a girl child is worth an education; my life story is the evidence. My story is actively dismantling the negative stereotypes surrounding the girl child, while also raising, coaching, and leading remarkable boys, men, girls, ladies, and women to positively impact their world. I have a place in this world, beyond just the kitchen, a broader place in the marketplace and society.

A story is indeed powerful, to form, reform or deform. I will take you through assorted styles of stories, which you can explore to share your story, the right way.

> *"The power of storytelling is undisputed, it's how we connect with people, build movements, and nurture cultures."*
>
> **Tyler Kelley**

TYPES OF STORIES

When contemplating on sharing your story, you may begin to ponder on the avenues through which you can convey. There are various kinds of stories, and I will be highlighting a few of the diverse narrative forms to inspire and guide you to share your own story.

1. **Origin story:** This is a story about your existence. You can share a story of your source, your purpose, why you exist, why you do what you do. For instance, the story of 'Why do I Exist?'

2. **Value story:** This story shares value systems, a cultural belief. For instance, a story on your core principles, the values that make you tick, a culture attraction.

3. **Vulnerable story:** This is a story sharing your vulnerability, this can be emotional, giving details of your humanity experience. Example: rape, grief, abuse story. As a leader in a charity organisation supporting vulnerable women, I have come across several vulnerable stories from strong women. These types of stories need to be heard.

4. **Personal story:** This can be called a personal narrative. It is based on your life's individual experiences, these experiences in most instances have significant meaning to you. It can provide great insight and lessons

5. for others. Further into this book, I will share various aspects of my life.

6. **Creative Story:** A creative story is a long story. It is organised, as some other stories could be an unplanned story. A creative story has characters and structure and helps to better tell your story. It can be classified into creative fiction and creative nonfiction.

   a. **Creative fiction:** This is a type of story that is made up, imagined, and not based on real life experience.
   b. **Creative nonfiction:** This is a story based on true events and experiences.

7. **Fairy Tale:** This type of story starts with 'Once Upon a time.' This is a classic type of story that brings imagination to life.

8. **Fables:** This story is represented by animals and or plants.

Foster-Harris, in 1959, claimed that there are only three types of stories:

1. Happy ending
2. Unhappy ending
3. Tragedy

In Christopher Booker's book, Seven Basic Plots, he outlines the seven typical themes that are followed by every kind of storytelling. He mentioned that most stories, if not all, follow these seven models.

1. **Overcoming the monster:** The hero in this type of story identifies an evil that threatens the land and determines to destroy that evil.

2. **Extremely poor to extraordinarily rich:** Known as rags to riches, this type of story tells you about a pauper, who blooms into a rich individual. It typifies a 'Rise.'

3. **The quest:** Just as the name suggests, the hero sets out on a mission, facing several challenges, obstacles, twists, and turns, along the way.

4. **Voyage and return:** This is about the hero that undertakes a journey to unknown grounds, overcoming all the challenges, risks all marked troubles, and returns a renewed person.

5. **Comedy:** This type of story is a humorous one, with loads of amusement and giggles. It has a happy and cheerful ending.

6. **Tragedy:** In this type of story, the protagonist is a villain, whose death causes rejoicing. It typifies a 'fall.'

7. **Rebirth:** This type of story is a story of reinvention, mostly starts with an awful tone and then gradually develops into a happy conclusion.

WHAT IS YOUR STORY?

In my professional journey, I have played the roles of both interviewer and interviewee, gaining valuable insights on both sides of the process. A common question interviewers/employer ask is, 'Tell me about yourself.' Undoubtedly, whether you have asked this question or found yourself answering it, it is a recurring theme in career dialogue. Even though the CV, which has the answer, is right in front of the interviewer, this question transcends the chronological details of one's professional journey. All that is desired is to know who the interviewee is; to unravel the core of an individual — their passions, motivations, soft skills, and the rationale behind seeking a particular role. In that moment, it is a prompt for a succinct pitch and an unveiling of identity — a means to capture the essence of the interviewee beyond career history. A means to set the stage for a more meaningful engagement.

> *"A story should be shared **clearly and effectively**."*

In everyday life, when you are asked: tell me your story, this simply implies that you are asked to share a brief history of your life. In other words, your background, what you have been through, and several events in your life leading up to this very moment.

So, I ask you, what is your story? You have a story, and you need to identify that story if you do not already know it and when you find it, use it, share it. In most instances, your story drives you, energises you, gives you the needed drive or push to carry on. Your story can be your why, even be the why you exist — your purpose in this world.

Your story is your past, your background, your origin, your values and what makes you, YOU. You have a story, reflect on your past, check your present and try to identify them (kindly pause, get a note) to answer these questions: 'Who am I?' The question of your Identity. 'Why am I here?,' the question of your purpose. 'Why do I do what I do?,' the question of your motive. 'Why am I doing what I do?,' the question of your drive. 'What don't I like?,' the question of your weakness. 'What do I like?,' the question of your strength. 'What drives me?,' the question of motivation. 'What is my passion?,' the question of your zeal. 'What are my habits?,' the question of your practice. 'What are my fears?,' the question of your concern. 'What motivates me?,' the question of your inspiration. 'What will I do for free, even when not paid for and will do pleasantly?,' the question of what gives you joy. 'For what would you like to be remembered?,' the question of legacy. So many questions, if indeed you paused, you will see where all these questions can lead you to. To identify your why and what your story is and what your story is not.

The bible says in Psalms 139:16-18: You saw me before I was born. Every day of my life was recorded in your book. Every moment was laid out before a single day had passed. How precious are your thoughts about me, O God. They cannot be numbered! I cannot even count them; they outnumber the grains of sand! And when I wake up, you are still with me! God knows you inside-out, before you were born and now, God has a purpose for your life.

People may know your name, but that does not automatically mean they know your story. It is easy to pass judgement on others, yet we often forget that we, too, are being constantly judged. Every individual carries a unique story, so it is unwise to form judgement without knowing the story that defines the individual.

individual. Consider your own narrative — What is your story? Understanding and sharing your story can influence how others perceive and connect with you. In human connection, attention is crucial. Pay attention to your story, others' stories, to know you and them. Everyone has a story worth hearing, you sure have a story. What is that narrative you hold dear? What is that aspiration you want to pass on? What is that story you want to impact the world with? What legacy does your story carry? These are the questions that illuminate the path toward a meaningful and lasting story — one that transcends the individual to contribute to a broader, shared legacy.

Now that you have acknowledged the significance of your story and you are ready to share it, consider these tips below to establish your story.

Top Tips to Establish Your Story:

- Choose to be vulnerable.
- Be reflective.
- Be grateful.
- Clarity - Be clear about what you want, what you do not want.
- Be specific.
- Be passionate.
- Ask honest questions, to discover the REAL you.

VISUAL REPRESENTATION OF HOW TO ESTABLISH YOUR STORY

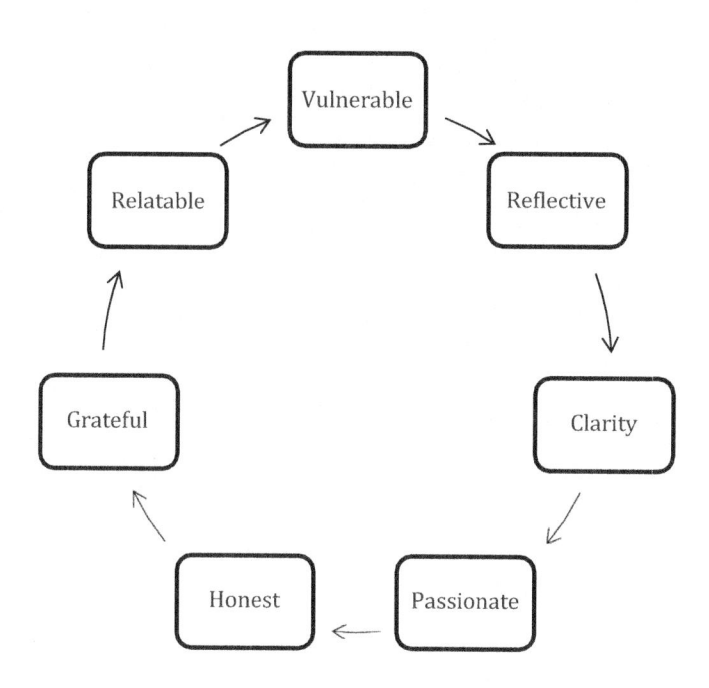

```
         Vulnerable
    ↗                ↘
Relatable          Reflective
   ↑                    ↘
                         ↓
Grateful              Clarity
   ↑                    ↙
    ↖                ↙
     Honest  ←  Passionate
```

When you establish your story, please refrain from denying any part of it. Embracing the fullness of your story is an affirmation of self-love, a vital component of your identity. Validate yourself as you express the beauty and strength in your journey, through this, you will experience true joy and confidence. When you take ownership of your story, you embrace both its strengths and challenges. This openness fosters a deeper connection with you and your life. It establishes the version of you that is authentic in this world.

Your audience is important to determine the best approach to share your story. When you have answered the question of What your story is, you need to answer the question of who your audience is, what you need to let your audience know and how the story would be shared to be understood by your target audience.

"The power of storytelling is undisputed, it's how we connect with people, build movements, and nurture cultures."

Tyler Kelley

CALL TO ACTION

▶ **Identify and Correct Misconceptions:** Have you identified any misconceptions or stereotypes in your life story that need to be addressed? Start writing today to correct them. Your narrative has the power to change perceptions.

▶ **Self-Discovery Questions:**

Take a moment to answer these questions:

Why am I here?

Why am I doing what I do?

What don't I like?

What do I like?

What drives me?

What is my passion?

What would I do for free, even if I weren't paid for it, and still do it pleasantly?

▶ **Craft Your Story:**

Based on your answers to the questions above: Define Your Story: What, now, can you say is your story?

Write it down!

▶ **Choose Your Style:** Decide on the style you would like to use to share your story. Will it be narrative, expository, reflective, or another style?

▶ **Cherish and Pass On:** Identify the cherished story you want to pass on to others.
What is the message or lesson you want to share?

▶ **Leverage Your Strengths:** Reflect on the strengths you can derive from your story. How can these strengths empower you and inspire others?

CHAPTER 3

Your Narrative, Your Strength: The Power of Personal Stories

> **CHAPTER HIGHLIGHTS**
>
> - There are several ways to share your story.
> - Your story comprises the pain, wins, and experiences.
> - Your background is important, it has shaped you.
> - Your story is exclusive, powerful, and important, even more, it makes you important.
> - You are the best person to share the version of your story.

WHO TELLS THE STORY BETTER?

A story is best heard straight from the horse's mouth (the owner). Nobody can tell your story like you, No one can give an accurate account of your story. **Your story is unique to you. Your story is a special message. Your story is your strength.**

Honestly, it can be a daunting task to share your story, especially the personal aspect. Your narrative, filled with various twists, turns, challenges, pains, and victories encapsulates the entirety of who you are. Your story is all of you. You! The idea of divulging your personal stories may feel intrusive, however, it holds importance in a world that often make-up individuals into someone they are not. Your story is a powerful testament to the battles you have conquered, it reveals who you are, what you are made of and the victories that you have achieved. It stands as a symbol of strength, bravery, vulnerability, courage, and triumph in a world that attempts to shape you otherwise.

A comparable situation experienced by two different individuals may yield different perspectives on the narrative. Your version of the story is important. Pregnancy and childbirth, for example, are unique experiences for different women. Despite being the same situation, they result in diverse stories.

Not everything that has happened or is happening in your life, right now, may be good. But the more reason you should know that God is good, He is a good God. An example of God's goodness is the life of Jesus Christ, his death, and resurrection. This gave us salvation. The devil may appear to be working overtime in a particular sphere of your life: marriage, home, career, education, health; it is in this deep darkness that the light of Christ will shine brighter. Unsaved–you need to accept the love of Jesus Christ. He loves you and can bring hope to that hopeless situation and cause you to laugh again and live to tell that story. There is someone out there who needs to hear and read your story. This may just be the inspiration, comfort, or challenge that resonates with and impacts that individual.

You do not have to be an author, actor or actress or a performer to share your story.

> *"Our stories have the power to break down barriers. Our stories bring us together. Our stories connect us to others."*

Your narrative is significant, powerful, and deserves to be told and heard. Sharing your story is about unveiling what is in your heart. By sharing your story, you liberate yourself from the burdens of the past and open doors to amazing new chapters in your life. In addition, your story can serve as a source of support for others who may feel isolated on their own journeys. By sharing, you not only empower yourself but also others. It is a transformative process that brings healing to you and others, comforting aching hearts. I once read that two things have been proven to help Holocaust survivors. Massage is one. Telling their story is another. Sharing your story touches lives and sets free. Therefore, it is time to stop procrastinating and share your story.

Your Story Matters. More Importantly, YOU matter.

Oluwajumoke Anu Akintunde

Chapter 3

– SHARE YOUR STORY! –

Consider this: many people have died, leaving this world at a younger age than you. You likely know at least one person, if not more. Famous names like, Anne Frank (died at 15), Princess Diana (died at 36), Aaliyah (died at 22), Martin Luther King Jr. (died at 39), Bob Marley (died at 36), Bruce Lee (died at 32), and Jesus Christ (died at 33). This is not meant to petrify you, but to emphasise the reality. You will not die but live to declare the beautiful things God intends for your life. However, these individuals are remembered because their stories were shared. The question is, who will know you and hear your story when you are gone? Stop delaying and share your story now. Make your life count, make your story count, share your story, and share it now.

Did you know that the challenges you went through, and your wins, some went through the same problems, challenges, but did not survive? Did you realize that you survived? Wow! You need to share your story.

TOP REASONS WHY YOU NEED TO SHARE YOUR STORY?

Should it matter if I do not share my story? I am not a storyteller; I cannot be an author. I am too busy to share any story. Do I even have a story? All these and more may be the doubts on your mind. Then, the strong points below should put you on the right track, reinforcing why you need to share your story.

1. **It fosters emotional intelligence** – When someone reads or hears your story, this can help foster, and regulate their emotions. Individuals can cope with challenging situations, learning from your experience. It helps individuals understand the feelings of others. It is like presenting a picture of how it feels going through that experience.

2. **It brings healing** – In the process of sharing your story, if it was a deep, hurtful experience, you gradually heal. Fitzgerald said, "Sharing our stories and being heard by others reminds a person that their life has value. It can
help a person see their life in new ways and can help to release tension or anxiety in the person." I recall a painful chapter in my life, centred around a loved one's diagnosis. Initially, I lived in denial, unable to discuss the experience comfortably. The emotional pain was so intense that even mentioning the diagnosis hurt badly. However, as I opened up to sharing the experience, I found healing.

Chapter 3

This journey inspired my determination to assist others going through painful experiences as much as I can.

3. **It can promote creativity** – Your story, when heard or read, can help individuals imagine what it is like to be in your shoes and empathise. You lend people emotions to re-live your story. This promotes creative thinking. Imagine hearing a story of a Canadian lady, telling you about snow and you are in Nigeria. The story fuels your imagination, enhances the power of creative thinking to comprehend what snow looks like, even when you have never experienced it. This was me as a child in Nigeria, Western Africa. I had never seen snow and only read this in books and could only imagine.

4. **It is a fun means of learning** – You can make individuals learn about a subject matter through campaigns, propaganda, drama, v-logs, etc. For instance, when individuals mention some cultural food, I may not relate, but watching a YouTube video of the preparation of the meal can surely help me learn in a fun way. Another good example is 'Show and Tell,' my children in Reception school years tell me about 'Show and Tell' stories they learn in school. In playing, you learn, and this can be fun and the memory stays with you even longer.

5. **It teaches lessons and messages for life growth** –
The nuggets derived from stories shared in a fun way are difficult to forget. These can be life lessons

transferable to individual life. There are several countries' meals I have prepared all by learning in fun ways. I remember watching a movie as a single lady titled, 'The story of my life' by the Mount Zion Faith Ministries. This was during my undergraduate days on university campus. After watching the movie, I became determined not to make any mistake in choosing a marital partner, a mistake could be fatal and life-destroying. Though a movie, the lessons stuck with me for life, and I have referred this movie to several individuals, generations after me.

6. **It can promote reading skills** – Your story, shared in books and or e-books, can indeed promote a reading culture. Readers are good writers, subsequently creating great writers. "You can't be a good writer without being a devoted reader." There are several books I have read, and researched on, that have helped me in putting this book together.

7. **It helps appreciation of diversity in our world** – The sharing of, reading of, watching, and listening to stories from different individuals and cultures can build versatility. Imagine hearing a story of a Scottish man's kilt, (knee-length skirt-like garment worn by men as a major element of the traditional national apparel of Scotland), from a cultural background where men wear only trousers. It will open you up to acceptance and make you appreciate Scottish culture. All these will happen without you living in Scotland or travelling to

Scotland to meet the Scottish.

8. **It creates innovative ideas – When** you share your story, maybe about a challenge you overcame, an individual is informed to believe and realise that there is a possibility, a way out of the same challenge they may go through or are currently going through.

9. **It can give hope** – Your story can impact the future of others. In a world that is filled with hopelessness, the least you can do is to give hope. When you read stories of past recession and how individuals survived, you are encouraged that any recent or upcoming recession is not the end.

10. **It can empower, impact life for good** – Your story is powerful, when you share your story, you share the power in your story, it can energize and change a life. It can give a compelling cause to live.

11. **It is part of humanity** – Your story makes you human. You are sharing your story to the people from a person who is characterized by diverse emotional expressions - kindness, compassion, sympathy, empathy, love, giving tender love, care, hope, to human life.

12. **It can preserve heritage, legacy, cultural knowledge and values** – Your story is for posterity, you preserve these stories for the next generations. Today, we encounter history and hear of several stories because it was documented by someone.

The film - Twelve Years a Slave, is an 1853 account of slavery by Solomon Northupas told to and written by David Wilson.

13. **It can lead to discovery of whole essence and purpose** – Why you are here on earth, what you are created to do, and the problem you are here to solve are deep self-discovery questions. Sharing your story can help
you discover it all–your 'why.' In writing this book, I have even discovered myself more.

14. **It can lead to business ideas/solutions** – When you hear business ideas, what comes to mind? Did you realise that your story can be put in a book, sang as a song, or dramatized as a movie? You can coach others, train others – a career path is an experience, and you can equip others.

15. **It can lead you to your ministry, your divine call** – I have seen individuals whose story led to a burden for a particular audience, and they lived for that reason only.

16. **It validates a point of connection** – It is an effective way to connect with others that share related stories, establishing common ground. This has the potential to make others, facing similar experience, feel less alone and make you realise that you are not alone. In return, they share their own stories, experiences, or they try to relate to your story if they have not had similar experiences.

Chapter 3

17. **It helps to validate your voice** – Your voice is unique and needs to be acknowledged. What you are saying is heard and people can see several efforts you have made. This will encourage you – your strength, skills, challenges, thoughts, and feelings.

18. **It shows a symbol of courage, strength, and bravery** – When you share your story, you can show the victories you have accomplished, the pains you have gone through, and the world is able to realise the journey you have been through.

19. **Your story inspires others** – Sharing your story will help you realise that it is not all about you. There are
several stories that have inspired me, some of which are: The story of Harriet Tubman, how she was enslaved, escaped and returned to save her family; Martin Luther King Jr.'s speech, 'I Have a Dream', delivered in 1963, inspired me and still inspires me, it is evergreen; the story of Deborah, in the bible, a great woman judge that inspired the Israelites, heard God's voice, and shared God's words; the story of Esther, also in the bible, that saved the Jewish from genocide.

20. **It helps you to let go of the past** – Sharing your story will let you let go of the past, no matter how painful it was. It will also help you to reflect on everything. You can reflect on how remarkable your journey has been, the high and the lows, the progress, and the growth you have made.

21. **Your story can bring people together and unite** – Your story can strengthen bonds when it draws people together. When you have gone through an experience, and it is shared, someone that has gone through that same or similar experience can relate. Such a person will identify with you through your story, and it will evoke feelings: laughter, tears, anger, joy. This can make your story a form of therapy and haven for people. Untold stories keep us apart. The reason your story must be told.

22. **It preserves legacy, culture, and heritage** – Your story is a form of identity–who you are, where you come from, and every other valuable information about you. **Your story defines you.** In knowing where you come from, you can know where you are going. George Santayana said, and I quote: "To know your future you must know your past."

23. **It can help you navigate the present and the future** – According to Gustavo Cerati, "Our future depends on how we understand the past." Nellie L McClung also said, "People must know the past to understand the present, and to face the

future." The Past is experience, present is experiment, future is expectation. It is paramount to use your story(experience) to navigate your present(experiments) to achieve your future(expectations). The understanding of the past, your story – experiences, can help you as the owner of the story to understand your future.

24. **Your story will create emotional well-being** – According to Emory University study, selected children were asked some "Do You Know" questions about their family history, and the data shows that the more children are aware of their history, the higher their emotional well-being. Also, the Emory University study showed that as children learn how their relatives lived through tough times, such as war and natural disasters, **they grow in confidence to overcome difficulties.**

"When you stand and share your story in an empowering way, your story will heal you and your story will heal someone else."

Iyanla Vanzant

After identifying the several reasons why, you need to share your story, the next question will be, "How do I share my story?" In the next section, you will read diverse ways you can share your story.

HOW TO SHARE YOUR STORY

Upon realising that your story is sufficient and deserves to be shared, as emphasised earlier, the importance of sharing becomes evident. Your rendition of your story can take various forms—book, testimony, song, blog, one-on-one conversations, etc., and you can share in a matter of seconds, depending on your preferred option.

1. **Social Media Platforms:** This is a platform that allows you to share your story in mere seconds. Across various social media such as Facebook, Instagram, Snapchat, TikTok, the 'Story' feature exists. This versatile tool enables the user to share their story through pictures with text, videos, or audio clips.

2. **Blogging:** You can tell someone your story by creating a blog, thereby earning you the name, blogger. In this digital age, a lot of people share their stories through blogging sites. You can also share yours there.

3. **V-log (Video Log):** This is a video recording of your story or experiences. You can tell your story in short moving pictures or reels by creating video stories. You can use YouTube or any of the social media platforms to share your video story.

4. **Author a book/E-Book/Audio book:**

▶ **E-Book:** This is known as 'electronic book,' a digital form of a printed book designed to be read on electronic devices or handheld devices like computers, laptops, tablets, iPads, and or smartphones. Several books that are available in printed or published versions can be found as e-books. These include everything from Fiction, Non- Fiction, Biography, Memoir, to academic texts.

▶ **Book:** This is a set of printed pages that have been fastened together within a cover for reading. It serves as a means for documenting information, stories in the form of writing, images, statistics, or charts. Typically, books consist of many pages bound together and guarded by a cover – paperback or hardcover. It can also be handwritten or printed work of fiction or non-fiction, Biography, Memoir, and academic texts.

Biography, Autobiography and Memoir can be referred to as life-books as they document real life events, mostly from birth to a specific time, in the life of an individual.

▶ **Biography:** This is your life history written by someone else.

Examples of famous biographies include:

- Churchill: A Life by Martin Gilbert
- Enrique's Journey by Sonia Nazario
- Into the Wild by Jon Krakauer
- A Beautiful Mind by Sylvia Nasar
- Napoleon: A Life by Andrew Roberts
- Steve Jobs by Walter Isaacson

▶ Autobiography: This is your story as written or documented by yourself. This is you, writing your life history.

Examples of famous autobiographies include:

- The Autobiography of Benjamin Franklin by Benjamin Franklin
- Long Walk to Freedom by Nelson Mandela
- The Story of My Experiments with Truth by Mahatma Gandhi
- The Diary of a Young Girl by Anne Frank
- Chronicles, Vol 1 by Bob Dylan
- The Autobiography of Malcolm X by Malcolm X

▶ **Memoir:** This is a collection of memories written by you, yourself.

Examples of famous memoirs include:

- Becoming by Michelle Obama.
- Angela's Ashes by Frank McCourt.
- The Liars' Club by Mary Karr.
- Educated by Tara Westover.
- The Glass Castle by Jeanette Walls.
- Wild: From Lost to Found on the Pacific Crest Trail by Cheryl Strayed.

COMPARISONS BETWEEN BIOGRAPHY, AUTOBIOGRAPHY AND MEMOIR

Memoir	Autobiography	Biography
The account of a person's specific experience by the person	The account of a person's personal life by the person	The account of a person's life by a third party
Subjective	Subjective	Objective
Written in first person	Written in first person	Written in third person
Focus on memory, emotions and not necessarily facts	Focus on facts	Focus on facts
Informal	Formal	Formal
Flexible research, and can be from own sources, more emotions	Focus on research from own source	Focus on research from various sources for accuracy
Nonfiction	Nonfiction	NonFiction
Specific History	General History by the person	General History by someone else

▶ **Audiobook:** This is the recording of a book to be read aloud. This requires listening to the book instead of reading the book. The reading of the complete text of a book is described as 'unabridged,' while the shorter version is known as abridgement.

▶ Word of mouth

- **Testimonials**: This can be a detailed or summarised sharing of the victories, and challenges that you have overcome. This can be to individuals(one-to-one), or group of people. I find joy in sharing my testimonies with others, highlighting the pains and the wins, especially, and then encouraging, giving hope to the target audience.

> *"The horrible part of your story will be the most important part of your testimony."*

- **Teaching**: This can be done by educating and instructing through storytelling. Great values can be taught through education. Deuteronomy 6:7: You must teach them to your children and talk about them when you are at home or out for a walk; at bedtime and the first thing in the morning. Parents are to diligently instruct their children at every opportunity.

- **One-to-one:** "This refers to a one-to-one discussion where two people engage directly with each other, excluding any involvement of others. It encompasses a variety of terms, such as one-to-one talk, one-to-one chat, one-to-one discussion, one-to-one banter, one-on- one, and face-to-face interaction.

- **Podcasts:** This is a digital audio or video file that is made available on the internet. It shares a theme, topic, or story. You can share your story through podcasts.
- ▶ **Songs and Hymns:** This is a musical composition of stories performed by human voice.

Examples of songs that tells a story:
- Voice of Truth - Casting Crowns
- He's Alive - Don Francisco
- Jesus Take the Wheel - Carrie Underwood
- I Need A Miracle - Third Day
- Rocky Raccoon – The Beatles.
- American Pie – Don McLean.

Hymn: is a type of song, partially synonymous with devotional song. It is specifically written for the purpose of adoration or prayer, and typically addressed to a deity or deities, God or to a prominent figure or personification.

Examples of Hymns that tell a story:

Blessed Assurance:

Blessed assurance, Jesus is mine!
O what a foretaste of glory divine!
Heir of salvation, purchase of God,

Chapter 3

*Born of His spirit, washed in His blood.
This is my story, this is my song,
Praising my Saviour all the day long.*

Fanny Crosby, blind at the age of six weeks, was a lifelong Methodist who began composing hymns at age six. An author of more than 8,000 gospel hymn texts, she drew her inspiration from her own faith. Crosby published hymns under several pen names including "Ella Dale," "Mrs. Kate Gringley", and "Miss Viola V. A".

"Blessed Assurance" was published in 1873 in the monthly magazine, 'Guide to Holiness'. Perhaps the biggest boost came when it appeared in Gospel Songs, No. 5 by Ira Sankey and was sung extensively in the Moody and Sankey revivals in Great Britain and the United States.

Crosby captured the poetic essence of the Wesleyan understanding of Christian perfection in the phrase, "O what a foretaste of glory divine!." The entire hymn is focused on heaven, a place where "perfect submission" and "perfect delight" will take place. The earthly existence is one of "watching and waiting, looking above." As we submit ourselves to Christ and are "filled with His goodness" and "lost in His love," we are remade in Christ's image and are moving toward Christian perfection. The refrain calls us to "prais[e]... my Savior all the day long," echoing

1st Thessalonians 5:17, "Pray without ceasing".

- **It is Well with My Soul:**
  When peace, like a river, attendeth my way,
  When sorrows like sea billows roll;
  Whatever my lot, thou hast taught me to say,
  It is well, it is well with my soul.

The only hymn ever written by Horatio Spafford; it was born from an unimaginable tragedy. Spafford was an affluent lawyer in Chicago with a large family. Then his life took a turn for the worse. Horatio and his wife, Anna, lost their young son to a fever. Then the great Chicago fire destroyed all his real estate holdings. Spafford planned a trip to Europe for a vacation, but he was called away at the last minute. He sent his family ahead, planning to take the next ship. During the voyage, a freighter broadsided the ship in the night, causing it to sink. Spafford received a cable from his wife, "Ship sunk. Lone survivor."

On the voyage to meet his devastated wife, the captain slowed the ship and brought him out on deck to see where his daughters had perished. He returned to his cabin, sat down, and wrote the words, "When sorrow like sea billows roll; it is well, it is well with my soul."

- **Just as I am:**

Just as I am, without one plea,
But that Thy blood was shed for me,
And that Thou bid'st me come to
Thee, O Lamb of God, I come!
I come!

Miss Elliott wrote the text for Just as I Am in 1835. It was published that same year in the second edition of The Invalid's Hymn Book, a collection which contained 115 of her original works. She wrote this hymn with the wish that it might aid, financially, in building a school for the children of poor clergymen that her own pastor brother was trying to build in Brighton, England. Miss Elliott felt so helpless in her plea to aid the parishioners in this laudable project. This one hymn, from the pen of the clergyman's invalid sister, brought in more funds than all his bazaars and projects combined. The brother himself left these words, "In the course of a long ministry, I hope to have been permitted to see some fruit of my labours; but I feel more has been done by a single hymn of my sister."

▶ **Journals:** This is a personal and intimate record of your thoughts, experiences, observations, ideas, wins and losses. This can be likened to a diary in its use, however the two are different. While the diary is used to record daily experiences, occurrences, and events as they happen, the journal is used for daily writing of a particular subject or a profession or record of things you do or see.

- Prayer Journal
- Family Journal
- Travel Journal
- Dream Journal
- Gratitude Journal
- Life Journal

▶ **Pictures:** You can share your pictures through picture collages, or photo albums. Arranging the pictures and adding texts in the chronological order you want your story shared. People can easily realise what you are trying to convey as your story as the pictures clearly show all the emotions, characters, and events that have happened. "A picture is worth a thousand words" meaning complex and several ideas can be conveyed through a single picture. A picture conveys its meaning or essence more effectively than verbal explanation.

▶ **Drama:** Your story can be told via drama. Drama is a written work that tells a story. It is a genre, or style of writing that passes its message or lessons through action and speech. It is meant to be performed as a theatrical performance, radio, movie, or television production. It is usually written as a script. You can share your story as a script without acting in the drama. Drama develops soft skills like creativity, enquiry, communication, empathy, self-confidence, cooperation, leadership, and negotiation. It is fun, memorable, entertaining, enjoyable, and visual. It encourages collaboration, teamwork, and empathy.

Types of Drama

- Comedy.
- Farce.
- Tragedy.
- Tragicomedy.
- Melodrama.
- Opera.
- Musical.

EXAMPLES OF TRUE-LIFE STORY DRAMA

▶ **Grease by Jim Jacobs and Warren Casey:** A Musical Drama. This popular play and movie tell the story of high school love between two teens who are completely opposite characters outside the love they share for each other.

▶ **Miracle at Manchester:** A true story about a high schooler whose bright future changed in an instant when he was diagnosed with aggressive cancer. But the power of prayer and support from his community renewed a father's faith and brought healing to a family.

▶ **The Intouchables:** A 2011 comedy/drama, based on the true story of the Frenchman Phillipe Borgo and his French-Algerian caregiver Abdel Sellou. Phillipe is an intellectual who loved life; however, he had gone through a paragliding accident that has left him quadriplegic.

▶ **Miracles from Heaven (2016):** Kylie Rogers had a rare, untreatable disorder that prevented her from digesting food. Despite the dreadful prognosis, her devoted mother, Jennifer Garner sought tirelessly for a way that could save her precious daughter. Everything shifted in that moment when Anna told an incredible story about visiting heaven after enduring a headlong fall into a tree. Her relatives and doctors were even more perplexed when the young girl recuperated from her terminal condition.

▶ **All the President's Men (1976):** Factually accurate film ever made.

▶ **Breakthrough (2019):** It features John Smith dropping through the ice when playing on an iced lake and failing to recover consciousness. Doctors warned his adoptive parents to prepare for the worst, but his mom, Joyce Smith, was confident that her son would recoup.

▶ **Eat, Pray, Love (2010)** American biographical romantic drama.

▶ **Sound of Music (1965)** American musical drama, a true-life story of the Von Trapp Family singers.

There are other ways to share your story via campaigns, propagandas, or games. At times, you may not want to be identified as the narrator of your story, you can share your story to an executive producer as a play or drama script, or to an author as a book manuscript.

In all, your story is an asset, which can be expressed in different forms, the diagram below further shows numerous ways you can share your story.

WAYS TO SHARE YOUR STORY

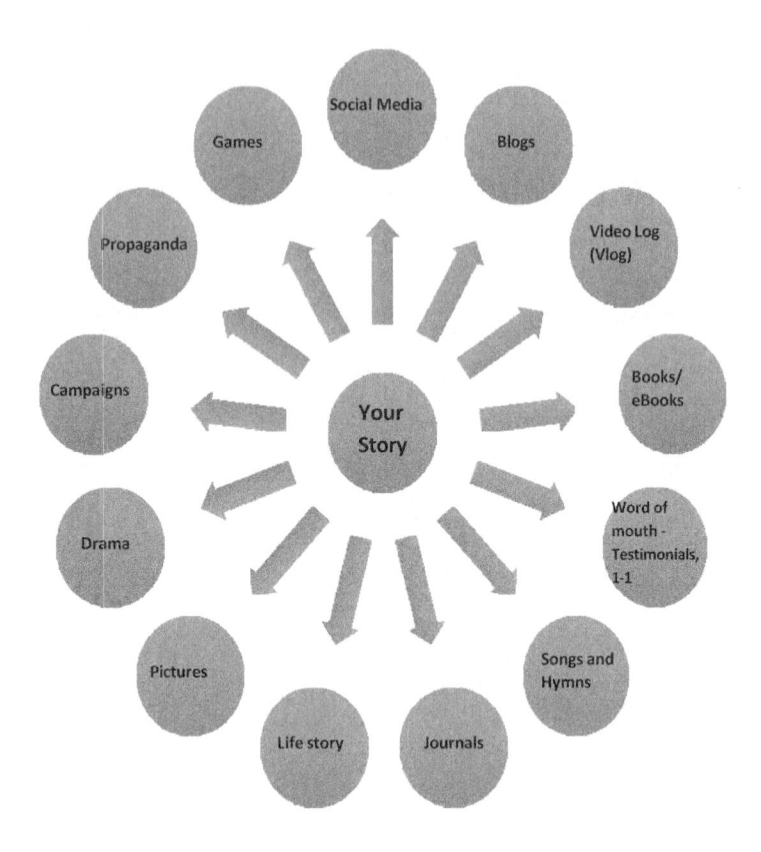

Diagram: "Your Story" at the center with arrows pointing outward to: Social Media, Blogs, Video Log (Vlog), Books/eBooks, Word of mouth - Testimonials, 1-1, Songs and Hymns, Journals, Life story, Pictures, Drama, Campaigns, Propaganda, Games.

In the next section, I will delve into the detailed process and progress of sharing your firsthand experiences, which encompass both your pains and victories. This journey of storytelling is crucial, as it involves articulating the various aspects of your life, including the challenges you've faced and the triumphs you've achieved. The diagram below illustrates how your story is an intricate tapestry woven from your pains, wins, and diverse experiences.

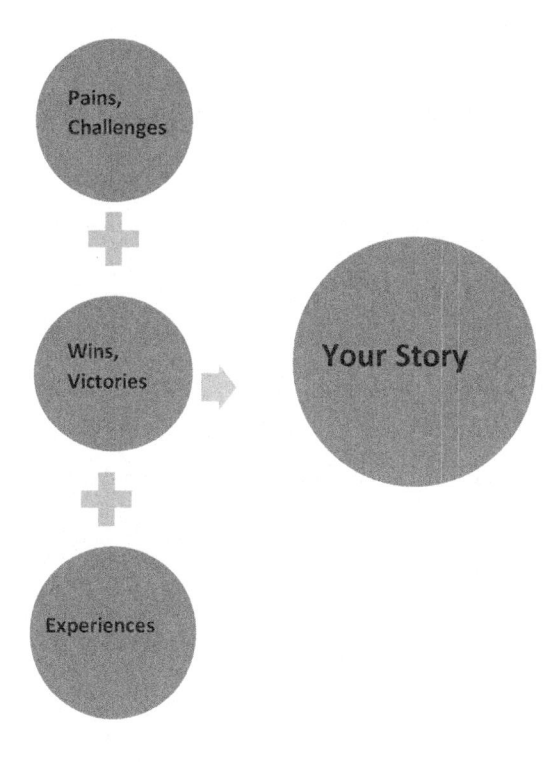

Chapter 3

Diagram Of Your Story

- Pains, Challenges
- ➕
- Wins, Victories ➡ **Your Story**
- ➕
- Experiences

YOUR EXPERIENCE

Your stories are shaped by your experiences. Experience, they say is the best teacher and life being a continuous learning journey, will give you experiences. However, over the years, I have come to realise that it is not just any experience that imparts wisdom; rather, the experience that has lessons to draw from, after thoughtful evaluation, is the best teacher. If you had an experience and you do not understand and extract valuable lessons from it, I am afraid to burst your bubbles, that you are destined to encounter the same experience, in a repetitive cycle. That is why in most projects, after the completion or in the process of completing, there is a recognized practice called – 'lessons learned.' Documenting these lessons is crucial so that the mistakes, takeaways in the experience or project does not repeat itself again, hence the lessons learned from the experience or project.

Your story – the journey of life is a big picture, which comprises several pieces, bits, and experiences here and there. There have been painful experiences that changed the course of your life, and helped you discover better ways to navigate the journey of life. Sometimes it takes a painful experience to make us change our ways.

Chapter 3

Blows and wounds scrub away evil, and beatings purge the inmost being.

Proverbs 20:30

Your experiences are valid, your experiences shape you. This is one of the reasons, in our professional journey, the Curriculum Vitae (CV), plays a crucial role to highlight our career experiences. Both your soft skills and experiences cannot be disregarded, they all contribute significantly to form a comprehensive profile. You cannot easily discard an individual from his or her background, as it comprises various experiences that shape who they are. Your experiences are real, you never let anyone tell you otherwise.

An essential part of your story that should be shared is your pain. As I mentioned earlier, your story is not complete without the inclusion of your pains, struggles, and challenges. In the next chapter, I will delve into the subject of your pain and the benefits that can be derived from challenging times, tough
moments, and periods of despair. It might sound surprising, but yes, there are indeed benefits, you only just need to reflect and read along and imagine, there are lots of benefits, opportunities, and blessings.

CALL TO ACTION:

▶ **Own Your Narrative:** Would you prefer your story to be told by someone else? Consider how much more authentic and powerful it can be if you tell the story yourself.

▶ **Identify Your Story:** Reflect on and decide what story you want to tell. What aspects of your life, experiences, or insights do you want to share with others?

▶ **Choose Your Medium:** Determine how you want to share your story. Will it be through writing, speaking, art, or another form of expression? Choose the medium that best fits your message and style.

▶ **Overcome Barriers:** Identify what is stopping you from telling your story. Is it fear, lack of time, or uncertainty about how to start? Recognize these barriers and take steps to overcome them.

▶ **Empower Through Experience:** Think about an experience you can share that has the potential to empower someone else. Your unique journey can inspire, motivate, and help others in ways you might not expect. Start sharing today!

CHAPTER 4

From Struggle to Strength: My Path of Faith and Resilience

CHAPTER HIGHLIGHTS

- Never judge anyone without knowing their struggles.
- Be slow to give opinions; you don't need one for every situation.
- Life has both positive and negative aspects.
- Life's journey, with its challenges and joys, is as important as the destination.
- Not all disabilities are visible; many have unique strengths.

Chapter 4

MY STORY: NUGGETS

My name is Jumoke Akintunde, I am fondly called Jumoke, Anu, and Jummy. I am an IT Consultant. I have over two decades experience in Leadership, and Information Technology. I am saved, redeemed of the Lord, I love meeting people and telling people about my hope, Jesus Christ. I am married, with three amazing children.

My story is my account of my fair share of life. My story is that of God's grace, mercies, goodness, and faith. I am a woman that has been immensely helped of the Lord. If it has not been God on my side, I would not be where I am today. I am grateful for the things I have rather than dwell on what I lack. Gratitude fills me. Everything I have includes my wins, failures, and challenges. You will agree that I cannot relay or convey the entirety of my life story in this chapter. Nevertheless, I will attempt to highlight various phases of my life.

I hail from the city of Lagos State, Nigeria, born into the family of Mr and Mrs V.O. Olusanya, in Ikoyi. I grew and spent most of my early years in Mile Two, Lagos. My immediate family was and is still the ultimate formation of my life. My family was a middle-income, religious, and morally grounded unit. Our daily routine included morning prayers at 6 am and evening prayers at 9 pm, marked by the resonating ring of a bell. Growing up alongside six siblings I acquired several life skills –

cooking, praying, respect, self-esteem, confidence, fear of God, resilience, and great business acumen. These skills, till today, have nurtured me into and made me the woman I am. Growing up with siblings and parents was filled with joy and excitement.

The house was always buzzing with activities, creating fun memories. My parents were intentional in their parenting. My mum was a teacher and retired as a headmistress and she is a businesswoman till date. My dad was an accountant, who worked as a Group Internal auditor till he retired.

My parents believed strongly in education. I already had my first degree, B.Sc. and second degree, MBA degree, before I got married. I was fifteen years old when I started my university education at Obafemi Awolowo University, Ile-Ife, Osun State, Nigeria, West Africa. Education was and is paramount and this amounted to my continuous learning and development.

I attended Ewe-Nla Nursery and Primary School, Oshodi, Lagos State Model College, Kankon, Badagry, Lagos State, a boarding school, and proceeded to Obafemi Awolowo University, Ile-Ife, Osun State, another south-western state, in Nigeria. There, I obtained a Bachelor of Science (B.Sc.) in International Relations.

Chapter 4

I later got my Master's in Business Administration (MBA) from Lagos State University (LASU) and Master of Science in Information Systems Management (M.Sc.) from the University of Liverpool, a maritime city in northwest England, United Kingdom. After then, I acquired several professional certifications in Information Technology – SCRUM, Agile, Amazon Web Services (AWS), Google Cloud, Microsoft, Oracle, TOGAF 9.2, Information Technology Infrastructure Library (ITIL), Azure, DevOps, JIRA, Six Sigma, Business Analysis, SnapLogic, Project management (Prince2) Software and Solution Architectures.

I started business as early as six years old, my grandmother was selling wares, and I would eagerly assist with customer interactions. Accompanying my mother with her business activities, I began selling seasonal fruits. Though it did not bring in many profits, the idea was not driven by financial need. I was ensuring that the fruits from the tree in front of our house did not go to waste, I would gather and sell them. Unknowingly, I was building my business acumen. Gradually, I evolved from an Administrator, Customer Service Officer, Bank Teller/ Cashier, Database Administrator (DBA), Applications Support Analyst, Consultant, Systems Analyst, Business Analyst, Data Analyst, and Systems Administrator to a Solutions Architect, Technical Consultant, in various countries, all around the world. It has been a vast experience working with professionals, where life-long relationships have been developed.

I met my husband in 1995, we were just fellowship members and did not start a relationship until January 2000, while I was about to finish my first-degree university education. It was a long-distance relationship, as I was in Lagos and my beloved was in Osun State. We did not get married until February 2005. Reflecting over this phase of my life, I can see God's faithfulness. I will break down these phases of my life into: 'before I do,' after 'I do' and still doing. Live! Laugh!! Love!!!

BEFORE 'I DO' NUGGETS

1. **Be yourself** – Discover you, know yourself, enjoy singleness, know God for yourself, discover your calling/ assignment/ purpose, serve your purpose, serve God. Be original, who God wants you to be, not a copy of another copy or someone else.

2. **Enjoy your singlehood** – Marriage does not have to define your joy or happiness. Enjoy every moment and make it count.

3. **When you find the lady or man, you will align, as she or he will find you in your assignment and help you in fulfilling that call.** When you are in your assignment/purpose, your spouse will align with that purpose.

4. **When you know God and you are sure He is the one telling you to go ahead, stay focused.**

5. **When you start a courtship relationship, there will be challenges.**

6. **Eliminate distractions, and world standards** – I remember visiting an uncle and aunt of mine and they asked, "Does not your husband drive." As at then, when he came on a visit to Lagos, he did not own a car. They already sized him up. He was not driving a car but had a drive (driven by a great God), purpose. Today, not only does he drive a car to the glory of God, but he has also bought a new car.

7. **Do not let anyone pressurise you** – Do not rush and do not let anyone define when you marry or not. Do not allow anyone to push you hastily into marriage, be the one to take the decision and face the consequences of who you marry. No one bears the cross with you.

8. **Eliminate limits, biases, cultural limits** – I remember when I was fed some biased statements: 'distant relationship doesn't work.' Marriage between Ijebus' (my ethnic origin) and Ondos' (my husband's ethnic origin) does not work', etc. To the glory of God, we have celebrated nineteen years of marriage and are going strong by God's grace.

9. **Do not keep up with the Joneses** – You do not need to impress anyone. Your marriage ceremony must not necessarily be the talk of the town. Do not impress and go bankrupt. Do not live a fake life. Be real!

10. **Believe in yourself** – Be confident in you!

> *"Sex never keeps a man – keep the bed undefiled, guys zip up, ladies close-up."*

11. **Sex never keeps a man** – Keep the bed undefiled, guys zip up, ladies close-up. Pre-marital sex is not God's will. Trying everyone in bed, does not help determine the man or woman with whom you are sexually compatible. No! It does not. When I was single, it was not fashionable to be a virgin but through God's grace, I stood out as a virgin. Know this, fashion will fade away, but God's word stands sure. His grace is available and sufficient for you.

12. **As a child of God, marry a genuinely born-again Christian** – Do not be deceived, there are wolves in sheep's clothing. There are instances where an individual will pretend to be 'born-again' and after the wedding, his or her real identity is exposed. Do not be deceived.

13. **Identify the red signals, and do not ignore the obvious red flags or dangers.** Do not excuse these red flags. Your emotions may excuse them, but you can do better by seeking independent godly counsels.

14. **Never think you can change any man or woman.**
You will take home the same individual you take to the altar. The altar does not change the man or woman.

15. **Marriage is not you** – Married or not, you are God's child, beautiful, and complete. Your marital status does not define you.

16. **Marriage will not necessarily make you happy.**
Your joy is independent of your marital status.

17. **Marriage is a demanding work**, be ready for the institution. The ceremony (wedding) is a different ball game from the institution (marriage). A lot of effort goes into the ceremony preparation, divert those efforts and energy into the institution.

18. **Manage your expectations** – Marriage is not all bed of roses, life is not. There will be highs and lows. Marriage is not a fairy tale, it is reality.

19. **Never marry out of pity.** It is your decision, be sure to stick by this decision.

20. **Make Jesus Christ the centre of it all** – The author of marriage is God; it would be the best practice to make Him the centre of what He created. This will help you, your relationship, marriage, home, and life, model the self-giving and sacrificial love in order to thrive.

AFTER 'I DO' AND STILL DOING NUGGETS

1. **Divorce does not have to be an option, God hates it.** Make the marriage work, try all you can to get the marriage to blossom before you give up.

2. **Identify authorities in your union that you can go to** – these are support or godly authorities that are unbiased and independent. Shout for help when needed and accept help when offered or given.

3. **Identify dangerous third parties, define, and set boundaries.** Your spouse is not your enemy. The real enemy is the devil.

4. **Marriage is for forgivers** – Your spouse will offend you, hurt you as you remain vulnerable to one another. Forgive! On many occasions, I have offended my spouse, and he has offended me. When you forgive, you let go, let God, move on, and wax stronger together.

5. **Trust one another** – Trust is a crucial element of a relationship. Build trust!

6. **Marriage is for givers;** I and my husband are givers and continually giving to ourselves by the grace of God Almighty. Give selflessly and sacrificially.

7. **There will be challenges and storms** – Forget the fairy tales of prince charming. Remember the

God of peace – Jesus Christ; He can still the storm. Invite Him to the challenge, let God into every stormy scenario.

8. **There would be waiting and valley seasons** – We all wait at diverse times in the journey of life. Waiting can be for a child, answers to prayers, an opportunity, promotion, provision, etc. What do waiters do? They serve! Just serve God and serve humanity. Remember God is with you always and He works all things for your good.

9. **Do not compare your marriage, husband, or children** – We are all on different timelines. Comparison leads to envy, jealousy, unnecessary pressure, and tension in your marriage. Avoid all forms of comparison in your marriage.

10. **Go on vacations, attend marriage seminars, conferences, and couples' programs.** We all attend training for our careers, businesses how much more our marriages. Rejuvenate, refresh, rewire, and renew your marriage.

> *"Your spouse is not your enemy.*
>
> *The real enemy is the devil."*

11. **Never think you can change your spouse, focus on changing yourself and your reaction to situations.** Change yourself by taking ownership and responsibility of self.

12. **A lot will contend with your marriage** – the society, culture, emotions, your career, third parties, challenges, even riches or affluence. Stay focused.

13. **Be submissive, one to another, serving one another, and accommodating one another.** Husband to the wife and wife to husband.

14. **Embrace each other's strength to the fullest.** Appreciate and celebrate the unique abilities your spouse brings to the table; you are not in a competition. Do not focus on the negatives, it broods resentment. Always keep in mind that you are not in a competition with your spouse.

15. **Be transparent, open; build one another.** The world has already done enough harm and is still doing enough to destroy godly marriages and homes. Encourage one another; challenge one another unto good works. Work together, two are better than one – harness your strengths.

16. **Live selflessly, it pays.** Marriage is not about me, myself, and I. Marriage is for givers, give selflessly. Take the attention off yourself for a moment, as and when due.

17. **Love, marriage is a decision, not a feeling.** There will be days you may not feel, but you stay true to your decision.

> *"You are not in a competition with your spouse."*

18. **Marriage is a responsibility;** you stay responsible to every phase of the marriage.

19. **Fight for your marriage, fight for your family.**

   > *"Fight for your marriage, fight for your family."*

   The world already devalues the family, institution of marriage. Fight for your marriage, children, family, especially on your knees. Fight!

20. **Guard your thoughts; there is a need to renew thoughts in marriage.** Be transformed by the renewing of your mind. Do you know that our actions are a function of our thoughts? What are you feeding your thoughts? The thoughts that go into a mind is birthed into a life. To change your life and have the best life experience, guide your thoughts.

Reflecting on my journey, I can see God's fingerprints all over my life and His presence, leaving His footprints in the sands as Jesus Christ walks beside me. What others may call a co-incident; I recognize as a divine incident (God-incident). If it occurs once, it can be an incident, more than once, it becomes an event. In my life, several events have unfolded, and I see the hands of God guiding me to the right places at the right time. I can boldly affirm that these are God-incidents, a testament to His orchestration of every moment of my life.

Despite experiencing the goodness and faithfulness of God, I have also experienced twists. I will share one of such twists in the next section and how God turned it around for good.

A TWIST

Opening up about my personal journey feels vulnerable, though worthwhile. My story, though intimate, is one I would love my children and grandchildren and their generations to read. It is easy to look outward, focusing on others, but looking inward has been both hard and rewarding. As you read through this book, you will delve deeper into my stories, and find lessons you can take away.

You might have already gathered that I have had several challenges, with one of the darkest being a diagnosis of a loved one—my son. As a mother, the birth of a child is such an amazing moment, bringing joy not only to the family but also to the world. I already had two girls and was just going to stop at two children. I felt no pressure from anyone, though my mum once suggested adding another, but I discarded the idea. But reflecting on how my brother had watched over me, even though he was my younger brother, and been a shoulder I could cry on, I reconsidered. As a young boy, I could remember how my dad would have my two young brothers accompany us on neighbourhood errands. It was 'a safe net' for us – the girls, so my dad believed. I vividly recall on one occasion my brother shielding and defending me, when a guy crossed my path, on my way to a local library as a teenager. Even as we grew older, I could call on him for advice and opinions on several matters.

All these and more reasons encouraged me to consider the thought of another child and hoped for a baby boy. I gave it a thought and later prayed to God and decided to try again. God gave my family the adorable gift of a boy and we were all happy and still happy. The sisters became the mother-hen. We all loved and nurtured him, even my dad, mum, and mum-in- love came over at various times to support me along the way. They were an amazing support system.

As our precious gift grew, he developed normally alongside his siblings. However, I started observing his discomforting reaction to noise, this caused me to take him out during noisy or loud gatherings – especially to church regularly where there were instruments and music. Despite feeling discouraged about going to gatherings, I still went along with my family. It was not until a visit from my mum that concerns heightened. She pointed out that he was not waving goodbye, not babbling, flapping his hands, and tiptoeing. As he was a boy, I thought his development was just delayed. My husband, acknowledging the same observations, suggested consulting a General Practitioner (GP). To get the GP, Child Development Centre (CDC) appointment was a huge challenge, but we eventually overcame it.

When my lovely child joined the nursery, he was blessed with wonderful ladies, who were extravagant in their love and support towards him. They were amazing, beautiful inside- out. They were very instrumental to his referral, Education, Health, and Care plan (EHC plan) and school admission. Prior to this process, the CDC alongside other health, and children professionals had to give us a diagnosis. The diagnosis was Autism Spectrum Disorder (ASD). In a bid not to give us (my husband and I) false hope, the doctor gave a brutal speech, the clause that stayed with me - 'he may never be able to do a lot of things'. This was a sledgehammer that broke my fragile heart. As a child of God, I rejected this statement under my breath and still thanked the doctor, as I felt the doctor was just the messenger and there was no point shooting the messenger. I wept, wept profusely, and uncontrollably. All I was offered was a tissue and the opportunity to stay a little longer if we wanted to.

You might be surprised that I did not know what this diagnosis was all about. Autism, what is Autism? During the medical chat, the team mentioned briefly what it was, and gave us literature for further studies. Many thanks to

Google (online search engine), I had to carry out an intensive search on what it was all about. As I read about the spectrum, it broke my heart, and I could see the symptoms all coming together. Immediately, we went to God's word (the bible), stood on the authority of God's word, and encouraged ourselves in the Lord. The word works, it works wonders. The word helped to dilute the toxicity from the briefing and assessment sessions. I knew God wants us well, as His thoughts concerning me and all that pertains to me are good. He is not a wicked nor evil God. I decided to fast and pray, depriving myself of necessities and seeking God.

I asked several questions, in my quest to understand and alleviate the diagnosis afflicting my son. I made enquiries, even reflected, by doing an inventory of what I did and did not do during the pregnancy. Despite my husband's reassurances that it was not about my actions or inactions. In my pursuit for answers, I delved into articles about immunisation - Measles, Mumps, Rubella (MMR), determined to link the issue to something. As a mother, reading this book, you know and understand the innate desire to be a super mum, striving always, to aid your child. But unfortunately, I felt handicapped, I could not help my boy. I felt like a failure, hindered from being the nurturing mother to my boy. The devil played on my mind, introducing doubts about my sin, parent's mistakes, or my food choices during pregnancy. Some individuals in the church said to me that it was my sin or the sins of my parents that caused it. The devil had free play on my mind. I blamed myself as I desperately sought to understand what went wrong. It was an exceedingly grim period for me and my family. I thought I would lose my sanity. But the good news is that I persevered and did not lose my mind. Here I am, authoring this story.

No matter what the diagnosis or the situation, I have good news for you, God is good, and incredibly good at that. Trust Him all the way, because to the glory of God, as a family, we are stronger together, overcoming the lies of the devil and triumphing with testimonies. Several songs, books and the bible gave us hope. For Me, John 9 verses 1-3, were so encouraging, especially verse 3 – Jesus answered, neither this man nor his parents sinned, but it was so that the works of God might be displayed and illustrated in him. I hope to author a book on this particular phase of my journey, in full detail sometime later. Now, my son is not where he was, he has improved, healed of several challenges. Though, I am still **very hopeful** and **expectant**, **eager** to keep you updated on his progress, **complete wholeness**. Watch out for the testimony report. By God's grace it would not be too long.

Taking charge, I and my family had to nip the issue in the bud, following the steps I have highlighted in subsequent chapters to identify my pain and find solutions. In the process, the pain has shaped me; I no longer ask "why". Instead, the question now is "why not me". Despite the twist, we emerged victorious, stronger, and better. Better days are ahead of us, triumphing in all.

I have had a reasonable share of victories, and challenges. There are a few I would share later in this book, but unfortunately, this book may not exhaust them all. Yes, this particular story might be the darkest moment or twist in my life journey, but I indeed learnt and gained knowledge. The situation was an eye-opener. I would be sharing a few, of which the United Kingdom system is one.

THE UK SYSTEMS

Living in the United Kingdom is filled with different benefits and challenges. The tax system may be stretching, especially if you are a high-income earner. It is necessary to contribute to the tax system. I must confess that the tax system is good, as it provides basic amenities and services to an average resident. It is like an insurance pot system that you contribute to and can access its benefits when you need it. My concern, especially, is those who work hard and pay so much into the system, but rarely get access to the system when they need it. The system allows for those that do not even contribute to 'misuse' the system. In the process, they make it unavailable to those who need the services and have contributed hugely into the pot. Let me further explain: You work from 9 am – 5 pm and rarely have time to get to the doctors and the NHS (National Health Service). When you need the doctors, the people that do not work or contribute have over-reaped the benefits from the pot than the ones that work from 9 am-5 pm have contributed to. To be honest, that is not a problem for me, as this keeps the society safe, otherwise these non-working classes will rob the diligent workers. Also, as an individual, it is good to take care of the needy in the society. The bible says, "Blessed is the one who considers the poor! In the day of trouble, the Lord delivers him;" and "Whoever despises his neighbour is a sinner, but blessed is he who is generous to the poor". My concern, however, is when the diligent workers need the services, the 'stay-at-home', benefit-earners, have taken all the slots; none left for the one that needs the slots genuinely. These benefit-earners know the system, have mastered the system, play the system, and even threaten the diligent workers. This does not present fairness; everyone should be made to contribute to the pot. Genuinely, I cannot generalise in this matter as some people really need the benefits and the support which the United Kingdom is providing, but there are a lot of loopholes and abuse of this benefit. Imagine, a tenant will destroy a landlord's house and will not pay the rent. Meanwhile, the property owner is expected

to pay mortgage, council tax, even if the tenant does not

Chapter 4

pay the respective bills. A young schoolchild of key stages 4 and 5 in the UK (ages between fourteen and eighteen by August 31 of the school year) is being admonished and encouraged to be ambitious. However, the child will tell you she or he is unwilling to go to university in order not to secure a student loan but would prefer to get pregnant to get child benefit and unemployment benefit.

> *Don't you remember the rule we had when we lived with you? "If you don't work, you don't eat. And now we are getting reports that a bunch of lazy good- for-nothings are taking advantage of you. This must not be tolerated. We command them to get to work immediately— no excuses, no arguments—and earn their own keep. Friends, do not slack off in doing your duty. Everyone is required to work, especially if able to.*
>
> **2 Thessalonians 3:10-13**

"If you don't work, you don't eat."

Bible.

As immigrants, we were faced with this horrible challenge. We had to keep working hard to remain residents yet barely had the privilege to secure the medical appointments required; the appointments were not available. The NHS appointments are only available when we had to be available at work also. Unfortunately, the time was ticking, and in this situation, an early intervention was key. We had to make sacrifices, here and there, just to get access to the needed services. Fortunately, my circle had its impact.

MY CIRCLE

My circle comprises my community, ethnic group, church, and all groups that are part of my life and co-existence.

The church is important to me and my family and was part of this phase of my life, hence the mention. The church comprises me and others of a Christian faith. There are lovely, God-fearing people in the church. However, the church can be likened to the hospital, where there are needy, whole, and challenging individuals. Some showed love and some were ready to judge and condemn swiftly, not minding the effect it had on others. Let us exercise caution in quickly judging others. You never know what someone is going through when you have never gone through the same path. And even when it is the same path, the experience is never the same. Remember, earlier in my story, I spoke about the same destination, unique experience.

Honestly speaking, some did not understand what Autism is. I would strongly encourage orientation and education of the church and other religious bodies. Especially, the church, as this was my experience, if the church has people with special needs as members, create

awareness concerning their health challenges and make provision for such individuals. Building infrastructures and services to meet the needs of these individuals should be put into consideration to allow inclusion.

There are some churches that facility access is not disabled friendly, you have clearly stated that such individuals are not welcomed. A church facility should have inclusive amenities for special needs and disabled individuals. If individuals do not understand an issue, a judgement is not required.

Some would mention to me that it would have been because of my sin, lack of faith and doubt. I want to make it clear that it is not all issue we must have a reason or an opinion for or judge. **It is important not to be swift to have an opinion on a matter.** I remember in some instances I get comments like, 'you don't have enough faith', 'it is your sin', 'your son is naughty', 'it is your parents' sin', and 'you haven't trained your son well'. I even remember an adult mentioning to me that you did not train your son well. He said this when my son tried to smell the food given to him. This is because he has a sensory need, where he liked to smell everything, and he was also very fussy with food. If the food did not smell right or the texture was not right, he would not eat it. To the glory of God, this has reduced, with social stories, prayers, God's help and substituting smell items. Then, we were on a journey, and we are all so grateful to

God for where we are now. He is a **specially enabled and amazing soldier of Christ.**

I remember that we had a visit from a couple, from church to encourage us at the time when they heard about the diagnosis. This was encouraging, comforting, and very reassuring. Also, there were several individuals who prayed with and for us and prophesied as well. On the flip side, there was an individual who engaged in gossip about my son's diagnosis, and a few, unfairly, labelled him and the family. I distinctly recall an incident when my daughters were invited for a play-over at someone's house, one of them asked if her brother could come. Unfortunately, he was not welcome and in response, my daughter responded that, "If my brother is not invited, sorry, I would not be coming over to your house". I was told what transpired and this was deeply emotional for me. His siblings have gone through various sacrifices, and indeed, that diagnosis changed our course as a family, albeit for good. Despite the challenges, we chose not to let it be a hindrance. Today, as a family, we are so grateful for how God has helped us. You need to see my prince charming, an incredibly happy chap. My warm gratitude to the siblings, carers, families, and all that have been part of the circle showing love and affection.

Many people are naturally comfortable with identifying with success stories, and in the case of my daughters, because they are neurotypical (have brains that operate in an equivalent way to most of their contemporaries), they have enjoyed loads of sleepovers and playdates. However, my son, being neurodivergent (has a brain that operates in a separate way to most of their contemporaries) has not been invited for such events, except during holidays or with family members. This highlights the different mix in our society, church, and social circle. Regardless of these dynamics, **God's report and opinion concerning the situation is what matters.** It is God's word that stands. He has the final say over my son. However, with unwavering authority and conviction, I know God desires healing and well-being for him. I am confident that he will fulfil God's purpose for his life.

As much as there are many diagnoses of Autism around the world, there should be more awareness on Autism and other disabilities for the society, Black African and Asian ethnic group, and the religious communities. **A lot of awareness is required for neurodiversity.** Diverse minds are an important part of humanity as are other types of diversity, such as ethnic group, gender, and race. There should be more awareness **that not all disabilities are visible.**

> Not all disabilities are visible. Please think before you judge!

If it had not been God, the story would have been a different instance. But with God's help, the church, family, and our circle, God has been our fortress, causing us to triumph. Today, we rejoice because God has helped us.

In the upcoming chapters of this book, you will read about pains, wins, and the revelation that a twist or challenge does not mark the end of your story.

You will discover how you can profoundly impact others through the sharing of your own journey. It is crucial to understand that facing a twist or being knocked down does not mean you failed; true failure occurs when you stay knocked down. The next read will guide you on what aspects of your story to share. You may feel vulnerable but remember that there is strength in vulnerability.

CALL TO ACTION

▶ **Be Intentional:** Identify the areas in your life where you need to be more deliberate and proactive. Make a plan to address these areas today.

▶ **Fight for What Matters:** Determine the aspects of your life that require your persistent effort and prayer. Dedicate time each day to pray and take actionable steps towards improving these areas.

▶ **Believe Beyond Diagnosis:** Reflect on any negative reports or diagnoses holding you back. Choose to believe in a positive outcome and take steps to align your actions with that belief.

▶ **Reflect Before Sharing Opinions:** Assess how quickly you form and share opinions. Commit to taking time for deeper reflection before expressing your thoughts on important matters.

▶ **Promote Inclusion:** Evaluate how inclusive and disabled-friendly your church and community are. Advocate for and take steps to improve accessibility and inclusion within these spaces.

▶ **Share Your Vulnerable Stories:** Recognize the strength in your vulnerability. Identify a personal story that could help others and take the initiative to share it with someone who might benefit.

▶ **Commit Your Twists to God:** Identify a significant challenge or twist in your life. Commit it to God through prayer and take ownership by seeking solutions and support, knowing that no problem is beyond His help.

CHAPTER 5

Unseen Battles: Turning Pain into Power

CHAPTER HIGHLIGHTS

- Pain refines and shapes us, offering valuable lessons.
- Sharing your pain helps others and turns you into a mentor and guide.
- Pain can unveil God's purpose and hidden strengths within you.
- Your attitude towards pain determines its impact on your life.
- Identify, accept, and resolve pain to transform it into power and purpose.

WHAT YOU CAN SHARE: YOUR PAINS

Pain is discomfort, hurt, ache, sorrow, heartache, grief, anguish, or any unpleasant situation you experience. Pain can feel like fire in your bosom, getting rid of an unwanted part of your life. It could be like a piece of sandpaper that is polishing or smoothing a piece, this piece can be your life or a part of your life.

Pain can 'feel like a Kick in the Guts'. This can be physical, psychological, or emotional pain. For physical pain, it can refer to the idea that you have a pain in your guts or body. For **emotional pain, which will be my focus**, it could mean you have suffered a significant emotional setback. You might have even been betrayed by someone you trust. Some examples include: a relationship break-up – 'Your relationship break-up was a kick in the guts'. Loss of a job – 'Losing that job was a kick in the guts'.

Pain can be challenges and difficulties we go through. Apostle Paul experienced pains in his life and confidently told the story of his pain to help us all. Paul said to the Corinthian church:

> *Oh, dear Corinthian friends! We have spoken honestly with you, and our hearts are open to you.*
>
> **2 Corinthians 6:11**

Jesus Christ went through a lot of pains, tests, and temptations. We know about it because it was shared. Someone needs to hear or read about your pains, challenges, and victories and be encouraged.

Let me share with you a popular story of the bible: Job was a man in the bible who loved God. He suddenly experienced several challenges (pain), and Job's wife told him to curse God and die. Job's friends initially came to give him succour, but when he did not get over his grief in good time or admit to any misconduct that caused the problems, they caused him more pain with their words. Then Job believed God had indeed turned away from him. The essence of this story is to call you to order; you need to be careful with your words. Are your words comforting or causing more pain to others?

Who can better minister to someone who has gone through divorce, experienced bankruptcy, faced special needs, or encountered failure than someone who has walked through that path? I want to implore older women and men to generously share their stories, serve as role models, and mentor the younger ones. I could remember attending a women's conference where young ladies asked the older women to come online and be visible on social media. The aim was to provide positive role models and influencers for younger women, sharing their counsels, personal stories, and nuggets. By so doing, they will be guided away from following worldly media influencers who are readily available online but without depth of godly experience. In addition, the younger ones should be receptive, as it takes two to grow a mutual relationship. Reflecting on the sacrifice of Jesus on the cross, we are reminded that he did not deserve to die. He went through those pains for your benefit, so that you could be saved; it is called redemptive pain. So, the problems, challenges, pains, and sufferings in your life can stem from various causes.

Some pains arise from poor decisions, such as neglecting to pay your bills and receiving a poor credit report. In such cases, you take personal responsibility for the problem. You cannot blame God for the poor credit report or the bailiffs coming after you for your bad choice. However, in some of your problems, you are genuinely innocent. You may have been hurt by the actions and sins of other people. No matter the origin of your pain, God can rescue you. Your pain often unveils God's purpose for your life. God never wastes a hurt; you should not waste your hurt or pain. Instead, you can use the pain you went through to help and benefit others.

He comforts us in all our troubles so that we can comfort others. When they are troubled, we will be able to give them the same comfort God has given us. For the more we suffer for Christ, the more God will shower us with his comfort through Christ.

2 Corinthians 1:4-5

ROLE MODELS OF PAIN

When you are going through pain, people around you are watching you. They are wondering what it means to be a Christian when you are in the same kind of pain they are. Does it feel any different? The truth is, we feel the same pain as everybody else. We just have a different source of comfort.

Your comfort as a Christian, is that you have hope, and this makes the pain a purposeful and less weighty one.

Apostle Paul was a professional at using his pain to model his message. He says in **2 Corinthians 6:4**:

In everything we do, we show that we are God's servants by patiently enduring troubles, hardships, and difficulties.

Your deepest life message emerges from your deepest pain. The world does not require Christians who appear perfect or have everything figured out. I certainly do not have it all together. What the world needs is practical, real, and authentic people—stories. They need to see Christians who exhibit patience amid pain and walk faithfully, even in suffering.

Every area of your life where you have experienced pain, challenge, or test is a testimony. Trial gives triumph, test gives testimony. Has God helped you work your way out of a health challenge or a difficult relationship? That was painful— but it is now a testimony. Has God helped you with the loss of a loved one? That is a testimony. Anywhere you have had pain and experienced God's help is a testimony. I urge you not to squander your pain; do not waste your hurt. There are people all around you currently facing the very challenge you have already overcome, and they need your help. They need to hear your story. They need to feel your comfort. Sharing your story is crucial, even though it is uniquely yours; it has the power to make a difference.

> *But how can they call on him to save them unless they believe in him? And how can they believe in him if they have never heard about him?* **And how can they hear about him unless someone tells them?**
> ***Romans 10:14***

The greatest witness of God's love in all of history was not Jesus' perfect life, his sermons, his miracles, or his parables. It was his suffering and pains. And His pain is now our gain. His precious blood and crucifixion paid for all our sins and diseases. Jesus Christ paid it in full. Even at the point of death, in His pain, He spoke in **Luke 23:34**:

Then Jesus said, 'Father, forgive them; for they do not know what they're doing...

This is a good model and example for you, to let go, even when it hurts badly. Forgiveness inclusive, He said 'forgive them for they do not know what they are doing'. Most people that hurt in most instances do not know what they are doing. Today, you and I are all good because He paid the price, the entire world is in a better place for that. God can use your faithfulness in suffering to a profound effect in someone's life. In fact, your faithfulness in suffering could be your greatest witness! Jesus Christ wants to use your story as a witness. If He can bring you through it, another person needs to hear and be encouraged that Jesus Christ can bring them through it also.

In the bible, we have the story of David, he had pains, challenges, struggles, valleys, and low moments.

Yea, though I walk through the valley of the shadow of death, I will fear no evil: for thou art with me; thy rod and thy staff they comfort me.

Psalm 23: 4

Joseph's story in the bible also is not without several pains – he experienced family discrimination, was falsely accused of rape, and endured betrayal. The challenges served to mature him and contributed to his growth on his journey. Jesus Christ had challenges and pains. He was tempted, he was betrayed, and he was flogged, humiliated, and crucified.

So, in life, we will have pains and challenges, even though no one wants pain. I do not and I know you do not; we all don't. Jesus Christ did not want pain, in **Matthew 26:39**:

And he went a little further, and fell on his face, and prayed, saying, O my Father, if it be possible, let this cup pass from me: nevertheless, not as I will, but as thou wilt.

Let us be clear on this matter, pain is part of your story, it is. You will have challenges. The bible says - For in this unbelieving world, you will experience trouble and sorrows, but you must be courageous, for I have conquered the world! - John 16:33. We have victory and peace in Christ.

Chapter 5

PROCESS OF PAIN

As hard as it may be to admit, there is gain in pain, beauty in ashes, triumph in your trials, victory in your struggles, and benefits in your challenges. Pain can be crushing, yet it is within this crushing that the juice of life is produced much like grapes crushed to make sweet wine. The crushing process involves pressure and in that painful journey, the crushing brings out succulent juice, beauty, and glory within you. The pressure helps release the resistance, unveiling the hidden treasures in you. Understand that the tough phases are part of a process. Just as there is night and day, regardless of the pain, pain can be likened to the 'night' phase of your life—the day (morning) will come. The day is likened to the pleasurable moments of your life.

It is important to emphasise that **God is in the process, not only in the promises.** He is in the process and the promises. There are several benefits acquired in the process. You are not made in a day; you are who you are today by the numerous processes you have gone through. I once read a book by John Maxwell, The 21 Irrefutable Laws of Leadership, in the law of process, he said "Leadership is learnt daily, not in a day". Leadership is not an innate trait, but rather a skill that is acquired through regular and consistent practice. He again said,

"Leadership can be learnt over time, and that willingness and ability to learn is what separates leaders and followers". You may think this does not apply to you, but it does. There is a leader in you, leaders are made through the refining process.

In your pain, **attitude is important**. Life is 10% of what happens to you. The 90% is how you react to what happens to you. Your attitude is essential, and it is your choice. In your journey of life, there will be challenges, struggles, pains; I wish I could tell you that your last challenge will be the last. But I am afraid to tell you, you may already know this, that challenges are inevitable, they are part of humanity. Also, remember, you cannot control what happens to you, however, **you can control how you react to the challenge.** Richard Branson once said, *"Tough times are inevitable in life and in business. But how you compose yourself during those times defines your spirit and will define your future"*.

Jesus says, *"You will have tribulation in this world. Do not be surprised by it, take heart in this, I have overcome the world"*.

No matter what the trouble is, you will overcome, and in overcoming you need to share your story, your pains, and your wins. Some of these pains need to be dealt with by the spirit and wisdom of God, especially when they appear in the form of challenges, obstacles, or obstructions. Ordinarily, your default response would be to attempt with human wisdom, but it is best to retreat, and surrender to the leading of God.

As mentioned earlier, nobody desires tough times, challenges, or disappointment. However, it's reassuring to discover that these painful experiences come with benefits, advantages, and positives, some of which will be discussed next.

TOP 10 POSITIVES OF PAIN

1. The challenges you go through contribute to your growth, strength, and development of your muscles. They foster resilience, resistance, and inner fortitude. Whether facing challenges in your career, business, Christian life, marriage, parenting and more, you may feel they are breaking you down, but in reality, they are advancing your muscle and resilience. For example: When you start weightlifting at the gym, you will start with lighter kilograms and advance as you go along. The dumbbells and kettlebells do not destroy you, no, they build you as you progress in the weights.

2. Pain changes you, opening you up to initiatives or ideas; it helps you to discover other paths to solve the pain. Sometimes it takes a painful experience to make us change our ways - Proverbs 20:30

3. Pain gives birth to hidden treasure(s) you may not have imagined existed within you prior to the

challenges.

4. Pain grows you; it matures you. Pain stretches your abilities and capabilities. Have you gone through a challenge, and you wonder how on earth you went through that phase. You thought you would lose your mind, but here you are today, you still have your mind intact.

> *"Sometimes it takes a painful experience to make us change our ways."*
> — **Bible**

5. Pain helps you discover your strength; how strong you are. *"You never know how strong you are... until being strong is the only choice you have."* - **Cayla Mills**

6. Pain can help to prune your life. It can help you to tighten up. For instance: On a dying bed, the patient identifies what is important and, in most instances, reconciles with loved ones, forgives and make-up with loved ones.

7. Your challenges, pains, and struggles can produce patience and endurance. The bible says in Romans 5:3: We can rejoice, too, when we run into problems and trials, for we know that they help us develop endurance.

8. Patience works out understanding and good temperament slows anger. The bible in Proverbs 14:29, says: A person of great understanding is patient, but a short temper is the height of stupidity. Colossians 1:10–11 explains how patience is a sign of strength, pleasing to the Lord.

9. The challenges you face can inspire you and others. It can inspire ideas in a bid to proffer a solution. You sure have seen individuals who inspired you, watching all that life has thrown at them, they keep pressing on—that is an inspiration.

10. Challenges help to build you to endure and persevere. A health psychologist, Shilagh Mirgain said, "we can shut down emotionally and let ourselves become hardened by it, or we can grow from the experience".

After exploring the positives of pain, you might be wondering how to recognize if you are currently going through a painful phase of your life. How can you identify pain or difficult moments? What if it is just a normal part of life?

The next section will guide you on how to identify pain and recognize pain points in your life.

IDENTIFYING YOUR PAIN

There is a story in the bible, about a woman called Hannah. She was barren, and a social embarrassment in the Old Testament of the bible. The pain stole her joy. However, she identified her problem, refused to wallow in her pain, rather got propelled to take honest steps of prayer and faith-filled praise. Her joy was full, and she had Samuel.

Pain is part of your story, as established earlier. It is important to identify and accept the pain rather than living in denial. What you cannot nip in the board you cannot address. Identify the pain. Pain points could be things that cause you stress, strife, or moments when you feel like things are veering off course and you are not sure how to regain control and get back on track.

GUIDE TO IDENTIFYING THE PAIN POINTS IN YOUR LIFE

You can identify pains in all areas of your life – financial, spiritual, academics, career, business, relationship, marriage.

1. Pain Audit or Assessment – What are those things that limit your maximum potential?
2. Highlight the root cause of the pain. What caused the break-up of that relationship? Given a second chance, what can you do differently?

3. What are those things that cause you stress?
4. What are your habits?
5. What keeps you up at night?
6. What causes you to weep?
7. What part of your life causes you shame? Or you do not like?
8. What would you change about you?
9. What takes your time? Could these items be automated? Could these items be delegated?
10. What are those things stifling your growth?
11. What is that 'Déjà vu' event? This occurs when you feel that a new situation is familiar. A French word for "already seen".

After identifying your pain points, let us go through steps to take to resolve the issues that you have identified. It is not enough to identify; you need to resolve the pains.

HOW TO RESOLVE IDENTIFIED PAINS

▶ Make use of available support and or help solutions.

▶ Leverage on existing solutions, you do not have to re- invent the wheels.

▶ **Learn from others' stories** – This can be e-books, books, blogs, v-logs, drama (movies), biographies, autobiographies, memoirs, etc. I have identified and come to an understanding that whatever challenge I am going through, someone has gone through it, someone is going through it now, and someone will still go through it. So, when I am faced with challenges, I carry out a background check or research related to that challenge. I make use of Google search engine, order books, read related stories, or an autobiography. This gives me strength to forge on. Most of the books I read give me a summary of several years of the author's life. Emma Thompson said, "I think books are like people, in the sense that they'll turn up in your life when you most need them". This has been reassuring and has helped me connect and know that I am not alone. It is not the worst, after all. "We read to know we are not alone." – C.S. Lewis

▶ **Consider your habits** – Instead of focusing on what you want to change, shift your attention to the negative habit or habits causing the pain and consider alternatives. I remember attending a few interviews where I faced rejection, experiencing pain in the form of disappointment, regrets, and perceived waste of time. The recurring feedback like, 'not good enough', 'unfortunately you were unsuccessful on this occasion, as there was a better candidate' left me daunted and frustrated. I had to decide there and then that their loss would be a gain to another company. I ask for feedback to gain insight into the interview process. Without delay, I substituted the pains with a better attitude. I once heard, "Nature abhors a vacuum", there had to be a replacement of that painful habit. Consequently, I replaced my 'victim' habit.

- Once you have identified the negative habits, you can create better ones that will help you rewrite your story, such as utilising delayed gratification.

▶ **Commit the pain(s) to God in prayers** – Matthew 11:28 (NIV) says: Come to me, all you who are weary and burdened, and I will give you rest.

Are you tired? Worn out? Burned out on religion? Come to me. Get away with me and you'll recover your life. I'll show you how to take a real rest. Walk with me and work with me— watch how I do it. Learn the unforced rhythms of grace. I won't lay anything heavy or ill-fitting on you. Keep company with me and you'll learn to live freely and lightly.

Matthew 11:28-30

▶ **Get instructions** – When you pray to God, it is a communication style to get answers and clear instructions to face the challenges. Listen to God for the next line of action.

▶ **This is not the time to moan** – This is not the time to apportion blame. Complaining or murmuring does not solve challenges.

Then all the congregation raised a loud cry, and the people wept that night. And all the people of Israel grumbled against Moses and Aaron. The whole congregation said to them, would that we had died in the land of Egypt! Or would that we had died in this wilderness! Why is the LORD bringing us into this land, to fall by the sword? Our wives and our little ones will become a prey. Would it not be better for us to go back to Egypt? And they said to one another, Let us choose a leader and go back to Egypt.

Numbers 14:1-4

▶ Highlight growth plans and strategies for highlighted pains.

▶ **Turn your pain to opportunities** – "Problems can become opportunities when the right people come together." — Robert Redford. Relocating to the

UK, my husband and I discovered settlement gap in the UK. Today, these gaps have been turned to opportunities to help others settle.

▶ **Identify lessons learnt** – There are lessons you can pick up from all your bad experiences and pains in life. What lesson can you find from yours? The lessons should be building blocks to a stronger and better version of you.

"Finding the lesson behind every adversity will be the one important thing that helps get you through it."

— *Roy T. Bennett*

▶ **Take responsibility! Take ownership!** – It is a hard nut to crack but you need to admit, what you did or did not do in the past and still doing that has contributed to where you are today. Looking inwardly rather than externally and blaming others.

▶ **Take your power back** – When you recognise that you are living for others, or blaming others for your unhappiness in life, you have given your power away because you are depending on or blaming others to make your life better. You need to take the power back.

▶ **Stop playing victim, see yourself as a victor** – Changing your story requires changing your perspective. Indeed, life may have thrown several challenges and pains; you need to decide to change your perspective and narrative. Your past is in the past, it is behind you; you need to choose the narrative and perspective of life your future will be.

▶ Tell your pain story in a different light – There are different sides to a story. Choose to tell your story differently. Tell your pain story from a different point of view. What benefits did you discover from that pain – that break-up, the loss, or disappointment?

▶ Have faith, do not doubt – No retreat, no surrender. Declare and prophesy God's word and promises concerning your challenges or situation. The bible in Mark 11: 23 says:

I can guarantee this truth: This is what will be done for someone who does not doubt but believes what he says will happen: He can say to this mountain, 'Be uprooted and thrown into the sea,' and it will be done for him.

Trust the process, see yourself to be able to turn your pain to gain, and change your pain into your power, purpose, and opportunities. You can change your tests to testimonies, trials to triumphs, and negatives to positives. Fear has an incredible ability to petrify your potential—to keep you from launching out and having confidence in yourself and life. To make progress in your life, you need to face those fears arising from the pain you encounter. Do not let the pain or past hurt control you! Your pains can make you bitter or better, you have the choice, you have the power.

ACCEPTANCE OF THE PAIN

> *"Every challenge you face today makes you stronger tomorrow. The challenge of life is intended to make you better, not bitter."*
>
> **– Roy T. Bennett**

It is important to accept the pain after identification. When you accept the pain, you can learn from it. You can embrace the pain and the glory that comes from it. I once heard – that experience is the best teacher, however, I learnt from a great man that,

> *"Experience is not the best teacher, the best teacher is the lessons learnt from an experience".*
>
> **– Dr. Henry Akintunde**

Acceptance of pain helps you to move on, opens the door to freedom, and steps to improve your life. The acceptance of the pain retrenches the power of that pain over you. You are now in charge and in control of the pain. This process is the reception and acknowledgement of the difficulties and challenges you have or will encounter. This will eliminate self- denial or self-deceit. What you do not accept you cannot solve; you need to accept it as a challenge to find a solution to the pain. Please know that the acceptance of a pain or challenge is not giving up.

> *"Life is about accepting the challenges along the way, choosing to keep moving forward, and savouring the journey."*
>
> **- Roy T. Bennett**

THE PAIN ACCEPTANCE JIGSAW

CALL TO ACTION

▶ **Find Positives in Pain:** Identify one positive outcome from the pain you are currently experiencing or have experienced. Write it down and reflect on how this has shaped you.

▶ **Evaluate Your Response to Pain:** Consider whether your pain has made you bitter or better. Make a conscious decision to turn your pain into a source of growth and strength.

▶ **Share to Help Others:** Think of a specific pain you've endured that could help someone else. Find an opportunity to share this experience with a friend, support group, or community.

▶ **Understand the Cause:** Determine the cause of your pain. Was it due to a bad choice or something beyond your control? Reflect on this to gain clarity and direction for moving forward.

▶ **Identify Lessons and Take Responsibility:** List the lessons you've learned from your pain. Identify areas where you need to take responsibility, and outline steps to take back your power from anything or anyone you've blamed.

▶ **Reframe Your Story:** Revisit your pain story and try to tell it from a different, more empowering perspective. Focus on the strengths and resilience you've gained.

▶ **Break the Cycle of Pain:** Recognize any recurring painful events (Déjà vu). Develop a plan to address these patterns and prevent them from repeating.

▶ **Accept and Own Your Pain:** Acknowledge a specific pain you need to accept. Embrace it as part of your journey and identify how you can use this acceptance to move forward constructively.

CHAPTER 6

Persevere to Triumph: Becoming the Next Success Story

CHAPTER HIGHLIGHTS

- One bad chapter doesn't end your story.
- Challenges are commas, not full stops.
- Trust God with the unknown future; don't give up.
- You'll be the next success story if you persevere.
- Use past wins to motivate you for current and future challenges.

IT IS NOT THE END OF THE STORY

You may be going through a challenging time or find yourself at a crossroad, and you feel like everything is coming to an end, leading you to contemplate giving up. However, I have good news for you—there is hope! Yes, there is hope even in the midst of your situation. Though it may feel like there is no direction, be rest assured that there is light at the end of the tunnel. You might be questioning the purpose and clarity of your path ahead, not knowing what comes next. It is important to know that there is a God that knows the future and knows all about your tomorrow. In fact, He has everything worked out and through Jesus Christ, he has a specific purpose designed for you. Yes!! He has a future for you.

Are you currently facing difficulties? If not now, there will be moments in this life when you will go through a few, perhaps even many. I wish I could say otherwise, but the truth is, you will go through tough times. Personally, I have been through numerous trials and still going through some challenges. However, it is crucial to focus on the word 'through.' This means that the challenge is transient and will eventually end. It is a phase, and like all phases, it will end. This too shall pass,

Chapter 6

"for our present troubles are small and won't last very long. Yet they produce for us a glory that vastly outweighs them and will last forever!" I have good news for you - We often suffer, but we are never crushed. Even when we don't know what to do, **we never give up.** *In times of trouble, God is with us, and when we are knocked down, we get up again... we know that God raised the Lord Jesus to life. And just as God raised Jesus, he will also raise us to life. Then he will bring us into his presence together*

2 Corinthians 4:8-9, 14

You may not know what the future holds, but you have a God – Jesus Christ that knows it all, He knows what the future holds. **Do not give up!** This is not the end, stay tuned, focused, and hopeful, so you can share your story.

That is why we never give up. Though our bodies are dying, our spirits are being renewed every day. For our present troubles are small and won't last very long. Yet they produce for us a glory that vastly outweighs them and will last forever!

2 Corinthians 4:16-17

You are never a failure until you quit, and it is always too soon to quit. God uses tough times to assess your persistence. It is not over until it is over. You may fall, but you do not lose when you are knocked down, you lose when you fail to get up. Wherever life may have knocked you down, I want you to rise. Arise!

> *"One bad chapter doesn't mean your story is over."*

Do you know how a little acorn becomes an oak tree? An oak tree is just an acorn that refuses to give up. Hold on till you overcome, so you can share your story. I have failed several times but that does not make me a failure. I fail forward, I 'learn' forward, and I push forward Your fear should not be failure, it should be succeeding in what is not your purpose or assignment. My challenges have not ended me. That is why I am still standing, standing tall to share my story. You will overcome!

When you feel like giving up, believe and trust in God's faithfulness to keep His promises. Remember that God's promises are not limited by earth's timing, He is not limited in time to fulfil His promises. He has till eternity to keep His word and accomplish His promises — His promises of hope, bright future, healing, blessing, and provision. Let those promises give you hope for all that God is doing in you, and for you — even when it is tough and extremely difficult. Hebrews, chapter 11, in the bible talks about all the heroes of faith and how they overcame by keeping faith and hope alive. You are the next hero of faith to be written about. Do not give-up, hang in there.

When something bad or negative happens that leads to an experience of pain in your life, you find yourself in a constant battle against hopelessness. You are inclined to think, 'This is the end of your story,' 'This is the end of your life'. But it is not the end of neither your story nor your life. It is, rather, the end of that challenge, a bad, difficult, tough time. In your life, you are going to have loads of challenges and pains that will end, but not your end until Jesus Christ returns. One bad chapter does not mean your story is over. Better chapters of your life await you. God is the expert architect and author of your story. He has the master plan and manuscript of your life. In the worst scenario, God brings glory out of the situation because He is in control of every detail of your life.

Let me create an illustration with the punctuation mark known as comma (,). The comma symbolises a short pause to separate parts of a sentence. It is not a full stop (.), a punctuation mark used to end a sentence. The challenges you are going through or will go through is like that comma (,). This is to tell you that your pains and challenges are not the end of your statement or story.

There are some individuals, at the encounter of challenges or hindrances, the instant response is withdrawal, isolation, building a wall around themselves to push people away. This is a wrong response because you need people, especially people of faith to trust God for victory on your behalf. You need all the support and help to bounce back on your feet. You need genuine godly persons to build you up to refocus on God. In the Bible Paul said:

> *because I know that the lavish supply of the Spirit of Jesus, the Anointed One, and your intercession for me will bring about my deliverance. With the support of people you let in, as discussed earlier in the section on how to resolve identified pains, you will overcome, and the pains will not lead to your end.*

Philippians 1:19

> *For there is hope for a tree, if it be cut down, that it will sprout again, and that its shoots will not cease. Though its root grows old in the earth, and its stump dies in the soil, yet at the scent of water it will bud and put out branches like a young plant.*

Job 14:7-9

In the next section of this chapter, I will share with you success stories. Stories of individuals who once failed, some failed severally, but decided to fail forward and today, you and I, celebrate them. These individuals did not make others define them via their challenges. They turned their pains to history and made their wins the story. You can also rewrite your hurt and challenges into your history and your wins, your story.

TOP SUCCESS STORIES

People that existed before you faced challenges, could be similar to yours. Some are currently facing similar challenges and generations to come will still face similar challenges. No matter how tough the challenge is, please do not make it the end of your story. The success stories in this section made it here because they did not give up; why would you give up? You should not give up, so that when others come after you and read your story, they can be inspired and motivated. Mahatma Gandhi said, "Be the change that you wish to see in the world."

▶ **Pastor E. A. Adeboye:** Pastor Enoch Adejare Adeboye is a minister of God in Nigeria, West Africa. He is a fulfilment of the scriptures

According to Zechariah 4:10 which says, "despise not the days of small beginnings." He is the General Overseer of the Redeemed Christian Church of God (RCCG). He said,

"My own rock was rock among rocks. My father was so poor, (that) poor people called him poor. The day he bought an umbrella, we were rejoicing. For the first eighteen years of my life, I had no pair of shoes. That is how things were and then I received Jesus Christ. Then things began to change, look at me today."

> *"You may fall, you do not lose when you are knocked down, you lose when you fail to get up."*

▶ **Mark Zuckerberg:** Mark dropped out from Harvard University in his second year. But today, he is a success story. He is a business magnate, internet entrepreneur and philanthropist. He owns several companies but the most popular is Facebook (now Meta Platforms). You are next, to make your own success story.

▶ **David:** David, a biblical character, was a man after God's heart. God loved him. When he told the king that he could kill the giant that tormented his community, he said:

Chapter 6

"Thy servant slew both the lion and the bear." He was confident of the victorious experience and happy to solve another similar challenge. Thy servant kept his father's sheep, and there came a lion, and a bear, and took a lamb out of the flock: and I went out after him, and smote him, and delivered it out of his mouth: and when he arose against me, I caught him by his beard, and smote him, and slew him

1 Samuel 17:34-35.

He had several victories from going to wars and fighting a giant. Irrespective of the victories, he had many troubles, so much that he wrote plainly in the book of Psalms, when the troubles overwhelmed him.

> *"The challenges you are going through or will go through is a comma (,) not a full stop(.)"*

Example:

God! Look! Enemies past counting!
Enemies sprouting like mushrooms,
Mobs of them all around me, roaring
their mockery:
"Hah! No help for him from God!"
But you, God, shield me on all sides;
You ground my feet, you lift my head high;
With all my might I shout up to God,
His answers thunder from the holy mountain.
I stretch myself out. I sleep.
Then I'm up again—rested, tall and steady,
Fearless before the enemy mobs
Coming at me from all sides.

Psalms 3: 1-6

Today, reading his story in the bible, it inspires. You can read many of his stories in the bible to inspire you.

▶ **Michael Jordan:** Michael Jordan is one of the most renowned basketball players in sports world history. He was a short-height boy early in childhood and was often rejected during the selection processes. After growing up, he started playing basketball, he even failed, missing over nine thousand (9000) shots, and ultimately lost over three hundred (300) games and 26 times. He was trusted to take the game winning shot and missed in his career. He said: *"I have missed more than 9000 shots in my career. I have lost almost 300 games. 26 times, I have been trusted to take the game winning shot and missed. I have failed over and repeatedly in my life. And that is why I succeed."* He got frustrated a lot, but his dedication and consistency paved his way towards success. He never let the rejection from his childhood selection processes or the failure of his shots or games he lost to deter his success story. The failures did not lead to the end of his desire to be the renowned basketball player he is, today.

▶ **Steve Jobs:** Steve was fired from the very company he started. This same man founded the Apple company; we all use their devices. His dismissal helped him realise that the passion for the work exceeded the pain in his sack. Steve Jobs said in 2005, *"I didn't see it then, but it turned out that getting fired from Apple was the best thing that could have ever* *happened to me".* Have you been made redundant, sacked, or heartbroken? You will be amazed how this pain can be rekindled to discover your passion and you would not believe, just as Jobs did not believe, that you can be the next CEO or have a better relationship.

▶ **Bill Gates:** Bill was a Harvard dropout. He co-owned a business called Traf-O-Data, which was a failure. Despite his failure, his skills and passion for computer programming turned his failure into the pioneer of the famous software company Microsoft. At some point, at 31 years of age, he was the world's youngest self-made billionaire. Today, all around the world Microsoft Office is a household useful tool. He said in his words: *"It's fine to celebrate success but it is more important to heed the lessons of failure."*

▶ **Henry Ford:** He was declared bankrupt before starting the Ford Motor Company. He was a renowned entrepreneur, who optimised and changed the United States automobile industry. Today, all over the world, the Ford automobile is driven and aiding transportation. Henry Ford's failures did not impede his innovation, rather it served as the incentive to refine his vision for a technology solution that would change his world. He said, *"Failure is simply the opportunity to begin again, this time more* *intelligently."* What is that thing that you are failing at and yet enthusiastic about? What is that business solution that would solve a problem? Why not simply revisit the opportunity again and this time you start afresh more intelligently, putting lessons learnt into perspective.

▶ **Thomas Edison** and his colleagues failed several times assessing the carbon-filament light bulb. Edison is known to be one of the greatest inventors of all time. His inventions include the light bulb and electric utility system, Electrographic Vote Recorder, recorded sound, motion pictures, phonograph, R&D labs, and the alkaline family of storage batteries. Despite all these inventions, he failed severally before succeeding. This should inspire you that you can fail forward or fail severally until you find a better way to solve the puzzle. He stumbled severally and when asked, he responded that he had only successfully found ways that will not work. Wow! This is having a good attitude towards challenges that could have made him give up. He said: *"Genius is one percent inspiration, ninety-nine percent perspiration."* He believed in hard work. *"There's a better way to do it- Find it."* Edison said: *"Many of life's failures are people who* *did not realise how close they were to success when they gave up."*

▶ **Albert Einstein:** He said: *"Success is failure in progress."* If you do not fail, you may never win. Most people know Einstein as a genius, but his life was not without challenges. He did not speak until he was nine years of age. He was known to be of a rebellious nature, and, because of this, he was expelled from school and refused admission to Zurich Polytechnic school. Yet, he never allowed these setbacks to deter him from winning the Nobel Prize in physics in 1921. Einstein always believed that success is failure in progress, so you should encourage yourself that no matter the setbacks you are going through or will go through; you will win, just like Albert Einstein did. There are several Nobel Prizes, medals, and victories still ahead of you. If you fail to succeed, who will receive all these accolades, certificates, prizes. You don't want to fail.

▶ **Walt Disney:** When you mention Disney or Disney land, Florida, or Paris, this brings pleasant memories, especially to children. Walter Elias Disney used to make cartoon sketches at school. At 19 years old, he started a cartoon motion picture company. But at the age of twenty-two, he failed and went bankrupt.

After some time, he created his cartoon character, Mickey Mouse, a humanlike mouse who typically wears red shorts, large yellow shoes, and white gloves which many children love and even adults. Today, we have Minnie Mouse, the sweetheart of Mickey. Who would believe that he was once bankrupt? No matter what your financial situation is, or your bank balance is, be encouraged, there is hope.

> *"At least there is hope for a tree: If it is cut down, it will sprout again, and its new shoots will not fail."*

Its roots may grow old in the ground and its stump die in the soil, yet at the scent of water it will bud and put forth shoots like a plant. Things may get worse, but as long as there is life, there is hope. God can make you laugh again. He has great plans for you.

> *"For I know the plans I have for you," says the LORD. "They are plans for good and not for disaster, to give you a future and a hope."*

WHY SOME SUCCEED AND SOME STRUGGLE

> *"You can make your hurts, challenges your history and your wins your story."*

As previously discussed, it is evident how certain individuals have transformed their challenges, pains, disappointments, and failures into inspiring success stories. These individuals succeeded despite facing formidable challenges. Conversely, similar challenges can lead others to struggle, experience depression, bitterness, resentment, and, tragically, even consider suicide. In the following, I would like to emphasise a few key points explaining why some individuals manage to succeed after facing challenges while others do not.

▶ **Lack of persistence:** Many individuals tend to give up after trying and failing, they abandon their pursuits after one or few unsuccessful attempts. Some give up just at the edge of victory. This lack of tenacity prevents these individuals from staying true to their vision. Reflecting on my own experience, I could remember when I relocated to UK several years ago and I applied for numerous roles.

I encountered rejections with a lot of 'unfortunately, you have been rejected on this occasion; we found a better candidate.' This got me discouraged and frustrated, but I refused to accept defeat. Today, the rest is history. I persevered and got my 'YES.' I only needed that one yes. I am glad I got the 'YES' and did not give up.

▶ **Lack of passion:** Some individuals are not enthusiastic about the situation. When you are dedicated to a vision or goal, you do not even know when time flies. "Time flies when you are having fun." You just have fun doing it repeatedly, till you get the desired result.

▶ In business, it is believed that half of businesses close in the first year, statistics state. According to the U.S. Bureau of Labor Statistics (BLS), this is not necessarily true. Data from the BLS shows that approximately 20% of new businesses fail during the first two years of being open, 45% during the first five years, and 65% during the first 10 years. Only 25% of new businesses make it to 15 years or more. This can be attributed to several reasons, see diagram below.

Reasons Businesses Fail

- Not satisfying a need
- Bad business plan
- Lack of financing
- Bad location
- Inflexibility
- Rapid expansion

Investopedia

▶ **Lack of self-worth:** A lack of self-worth can make you undermine yourself. You can feel the challenge is the end of the world, thinking you cannot overcome or pass through the challenge or difficulty.

▶ **Lack of right mind-set:** When you have the right mind-set, you will embrace challenges and discover opportunities amid problems. You will stay resilient and resolute in your tough times. The right mind-set is vital to a good life, wellbeing, health, body, relationships, career, business, and life success. For example, when you attend an interview with the right mind-set, but you do not get the job, do you just accept that 'you were not good enough?' or 'the company didn't deserve you' or 'there is a better company out there waiting for you.' Do you try to know why you did not get the job offer, ask for feedback, develop yourself and get ready for another job interview. Get your mind-set right, a 'growth mind- set.' When demeaning, negative thoughts come to mind, learn to kill the thoughts immediately. Be an assassinator of negative, demeaning thoughts instantly.

THE GROWTH MIND-SET TABLE

Fixed Mindset	Growth Mindset
Feedback is a personal attachment	Feedback is key and helps grow
Too hard, give up	Keep trying in hard, tough moments
Success threatens	Success inspires
Dislike challenges	Likes challenges and sees opportunities
Focus on proving self	Focus on process, not result
Avoid unfamiliar zones	Step out of comfort zone

"When you have the right mindset you embrace challenges, discover opportunities amid problems."

▶ **Lack of ownership:** In most instances, you blame others for your problems, rather than look inward to identify what you could have done better to avoid the challenge. All you have to do is identify your pain points, focus, and grow from the lessons gained from the situation and make that situation better. You can discover opportunities from the situation and make a success story out of it. I am mindful that, at times, individuals can contribute to the challenges, but the key is to take ownership. When you blame others, you have given the responsibility to control the problem to that individual. How do you blame others? For example: your money was stolen by your employee. Rather than blame the employee, you can look internally: how did I employ a criminal? Check the recruitment process. Are any checks conducted before employment? Are any references provided or filed? Who has access to funds? What are the security measures? etc. Rather than let the theft cause you so much loss, you can think on the lessons learnt and take steps to avoid similar occurrences in the future or manage the crisis and see if there are remedial actions to recover the funds.

▶ **Lack of reflection:** When challenges come your way, rather than getting overwhelmed, you can reflect on and identify past victories and draw strength from those victories. A good example I shared earlier is the story of David when he remembered his past victories of killing a bear and lion while tending his father's flock. This reflection gave him the confidence and courage needed, that he could kill the giant, Goliath. Reflect! In challenging times.

▶ **Comparison:** This is the consideration and estimation of the similarities or differences between you and someone else. You are on a different journey path from that other person. Comparison can create undue stress and bring pressure to your journey. You do not need the extra baggage in your journey of life. "Stop comparing yourself to other people: you are an original. We are all different and it's okay." - Joyce Meyer. Have you noticed that on social media, most people post their best pictures, certain individuals, even post 'photo-shopped' pictures and fake lifestyles. So, why mount undue pressure on yourself by comparing a 'fake life' with your reality?

"No one can make you feel inferior without your consent."

Eleanor Roosevelt

Never let anyone make you feel inferior or inadequate, you are unique. Identify your triggers for comparison, once identified, avoid them. For your emotional and mental well-being, use comparison as an improvement catalyst and motivation, your past as comparison to measure your growth, celebrate and rejoice in others' wins, count your blessings, name them, and meditate on the blessings, spend less time on or avoid social media. Have that self-awareness that 'money isn't everything,' 'all that glitters is not gold'.

▶ **Fear:** Fear is the opposite of Faith. Growing up, there was a mnemonic for fear - False Evidence Appearing Real. The challenges are fake, temporal, and just appearing real, so why allow a temporal situation to collapse you? Fear can lead to several mental disorders, anxiety, even death. For instance, during COVID, a lot of people died just out of fear. A research, on a total of 1840 participants in Lebanon, was included in the analysis of which 62.9% were females and 62.2% were single. The age of the participants ranged from 18 to 70 years with a mean of 26.6 ±8.8 years. Of the total participants, 41.9% felt uncomfortable thinking about the novel Coronavirus and 35.4% of candidates became nervous or anxious when watching the news about COVID-19 on social media. About one-third of the participants (33.7%)

were afraid of COVID-19 and 23.8% were afraid of losing their lives because of the disease. Concerning somatic symptoms of fear, 7.9% reported increased heart races or palpitations whenever they thought about getting infected with COVID-19, 3.7% complained about sleep disturbances while 2.5% developed tremors or sweating in their hands when they thought about Coronavirus. In addition, death anxiety related to the COVID-19 pandemic was one of the most fear-related factors (B = 0.191, 95% CI (0.172 to 0.211), P-value < 0.0001).

In other words, you need faith to counter fear. How do you get faith: faith comes by hearing and hearing God's word. How do I get God's words? You can get them in the book called the Bible. The Bible says in Romans 10:17, *"So then faith comes by hearing, and hearing by the word of God."* The word of God gives hope in hopelessness and faith irrespective of fear. The words are true! Tried and assessed.

I have benefitted enormously from these real and living words, the bible, personally.

▶ **Denying available help:** At times, you can be amid solutions to your problems and not realise. There are support systems all over, identify one for your situation and use the support system. You can find a support system in a church community, family, professional support system, well-being group, and most importantly with God. I once read: Psalms 121, which says: *"I lift my eyes to the hills.... where does my help come from? My help comes from the LORD..."* A song artist, The Brooklyn Tabernacle Choir, once sang – My Help Cometh from the Lord.

LYRICS:

*I will lift up mine eyes to the hills. From whence cometh my help. My help cometh from the Lord, The Lord which made heaven and earth. He said, He would not suffer thy foot, Thy foot to be moved.
The Lord that keepeth thee, He will not slumber nor sleep.*

Oh, the Lord is thy keeper, the Lord is thy shade. Upon thy right hand, upon thy right hand.
No, the sun shall not smite thee by day,
Nor the moon by night. He shall preserve thy soul, even forevermore.

My help, my help, my help,
All of my help cometh from the Lord. Gonna keep my eyes on You Lord.
I won't look to the left, I won't look to right. I'll stay focused on You Jesus.
I lift up my eyes, I look to the hills (He is my strength). All of my help cometh from the Lord.

Chapter 6

CALL TO ACTION

▶ **Turn Pain into Purpose:** Reflect on a painful experience you've had. Decide to transform it into a story and share it. What story can you tell from this pain?

▶ **Create a Message from Your Mess:** Identify a difficult situation you've faced. How can you turn this mess into a meaningful message for others?

▶ **Learn from Failures:** List the lessons you've learned from your failures. How can these lessons guide you moving forward?

▶ **Voice Your Passion:** Identify what you are passionate about and find a way to express it. The world is waiting to hear your voice. What steps can you take today to give your passion a voice?

▶ **Stop Procrastinating:** Recognize on what you've been procrastinating. Commit to ending procrastination
and take immediate action to make your life count. What task can you tackle right now?

▶ **Grow Your Faith:** Consider ways to deepen your faith. What practices or activities can you engage in to strengthen your belief and trust?

▶ **Face Your Fears:** Identify your fears. What steps can you take to confront and overcome them?

CHAPTER 7

Celebrate and Share: The Power of Your Victories

CHAPTER HIGHLIGHTS

- Your victories are part of your story, share them.
- There are positives and benefits in your success story.
- Celebrate your victories, some people are desperate for those wins.
- You need to exercise caution in your wins, so you do not experience pitfalls.
- You need to document your wins, they are the inspiration for tomorrow.

WHAT YOU CAN SHARE: YOUR VICTORIES

In writing your story, as much as you have challenges, pains, and difficulties; you must be honest and grateful to recognize your victories, your triumphs, your conquests, your wins, and your successes. All these are part of your story, which without, your story is incomplete. Life can be likened to a coin, both sides of it make it the coin.

> *"The two sides of life – the pains and wins come together to be your story."*

These triumphs empower you and others to forge ahead and take adventure into more territories. I remember, again, the story of David, in the bible. He helps his father on the fields, to look after his father's flock. Several times, other animals attempted to kill the flock he was keeping, and he killed a bear and also a lion. These acts gave him confidence to offer to kill a giant that was intimidating his community. When he offered to kill the giant, the community king asked, are you sure you can kill this giant? He said that he had killed a bear, and a lion, and the God that helped him with those animals is able to help him defeat the giant. You can see in this story how the confidence gained from previous wins energised him and strengthened him to kill the giant that everyone dreaded. That is how your win empowers you and others, especially when it is shared.

In my life, I have experienced a few economic recessions, the victories recorded from these recessions encouraged me that no matter the economic downtime, the God that saw me through, will sure see me through any other one. It is therefore important to receive God's grace, to see the blessings in your mess.

DISCOVER THE POSITIVES OF VICTORIES

It is good practice to acknowledge and celebrate your small and big wins or victories. Research shows that celebrating your wins can increase your innate motivation, which is the drive to pursue more of your goals and it is rewarding, refreshing, self-satisfying and fulfilling. If you can, journal every win, never cheapen any win, or claim it is a coincidence. A win or victory is worth recognizing.

> *"Your wins are someone else's prayer points."*

Where you are now is another person's desire. Do not take it for granted.

1. Victories encourage you to achieve more.
2. Wins develop your confidence.
3. The wins, motivates and inspires you to take giant strides.
4. Your wins inspire others, give hope, and empower others.
5. Victories develop resilience, the ability to survive challenges, pains, disappointments, and tough times.
6. Your wins will help you to attain your desired goals – short-term or long-term goals.
7. Your successes can elevate your self-esteem, self-worth.
8. Your victories can help your mental well-being. Success or failure does not define you, however your successes lead to happiness, which can help your mental health, eliminating negative feelings and thoughts and its effect.
9. Your victories support your society. When you win, it is a benefit to humanity.
10. Your wins open doors and take you to another dimension of opportunities.

In excelling, you must exercise due caution not to fall in ditches that may come along with success. I will bring your attention to mistakes to avoid in your wins.

Chapter 7

MISTAKES TO AVOID IN WINS

Most things that have benefits in life tend to also have drawbacks, these are victories caveats. In this section, I will discuss some caveats you need to look out for in celebrating wins.

▶ **Burn out:** Celebrating wins can lead to burnout because the reward of hard work in most instances is more work. You need to exercise caution not to burn out. As this comes with feelings of depression, anxiety, and stress.

▶ **Fear of popularity:** Some individuals fear the status of a celebrity. This is because there are challenges that come with popularity: the loss of privacy, being in the eyes of the public, media publicity and its fake reports, etc. Hence, some individuals avoid making giant strides that could lead to being noticed.

▶ **Diarize your appointments:** Dennis Najjar said, "As an entrepreneur, I get things done by sticking to one rule: Scheduling and organising everything I commit to. It might sound like an easy decision, but most people fail to do this. If you can get into the rhythm of assigning yourself tasks and calendar appointments, you will never find yourself struggling to remember all the things you already forgot at 3 a.m.".

▶ **Trying to please everyone:** You want approval from others, fair enough, and you want to be liked. When you succeed and you want to stay a success, you cannot please everyone, everyone has an opinion. This can set you back.

▶ **Pride:** After several wins and victories, you need to be cautious about pride. Avoid arrogance, it will lead to destruction, it can come as a fall or a loss. It is a thin line to cross from self-esteem to self-importance, after many victories and applause. Pride made Lucifer fall; pride plummeted a lot of victorious people that did not exercise caution. It is important that you humble yourself.

▶ **Not setting boundaries:** Boundaries are important if you want to learn the art of affirming pushbacks. Winning challenges and known to have won challenges can lead to a lot of patronising. However, you should be firm with your boundaries and how far you can go on your freewill. Know your limits, insist on it and work with it. You want to set healthy boundaries; this will help your health and sanity, as a whole. The reward of hard work, I say, is more work. As such, you want to be able to clearly say – 'enough is enough.'

▶ **Do not take it for granted, celebrate:** Do not forget the goodness of God as you claim the wins. Fix your eyes on Jesus Christ and the promises of God. Keep a journal of His divine intervention, His hands at work in an unexplainable way in your ministry, career, marriage, or life. When fear sets in and you get anxious about anything, you can read through the journal to affirm that God can do it again. However, when you feel fear, it is alright, but never let it overwhelm you—Fear can make you forget all the goodness of God. Remind yourself of these victories, reflect on them and keep your eyes on the God of the victories.

▶ **Not asking for help:** You need people, you need other's resources, and others need you. Give a lending hand when you can. Although, you need to be clear in your request for help as required. Ask Jesus Christ for help when you need to. God can give you supernatural strength to achieve greater heights. The one that called you can equip you with all you need for the journey.

▶ **Lack of good character:** This is the absence of expected values in exchange for unacceptable behaviours. Oscar Levant said: "Underneath this flabby exterior is an enormous lack of character." The lack of good character can impact victories on all sides of life.

"The difference between a successful person and others is not a lack of strength, not a lack of knowledge, but rather a lack of will."

Vince Lombardi.

It reduces your self-worth and when that is reduced, most, if not all, lose respect for you and failure is inevitable.

▶ **Lack of integrity:** This is the inability to stay true to a good ethical behaviour irrespective of external pressure. This can include not keeping to promises, appointments and not paying your debts and bills. Not paying your bills and debts can damage your credit score and close some financial doors. Do you spend money on what you want and not what you need? Thereby leading you to spend more than you earn? Buy now, pay later? You need to control your appetite. When you owe, pay up, it is a lack of integrity and wickedness to owe and not pay up.

The wicked borrow and never pay back.

Psalm 37:21.

When you agree to an appointment, respect others' time, and keep to your words and promises.

People who promise things that they never give are like clouds and wind that bring no rain.

Proverbs 25:14.

A lot idolise success, it is incredibly good to uphold and celebrate success stories, your victories, and wins. However, when and if at any point, you succeed and, by any chance, you fail, it is not the end of you, not the end of the world — humans make mistakes.

There is no one on earth who does what is right all the time and never makes a mistake.

Ecclesiastes 7:20.

CALL TO ACTION

▶ **Seek Support:** Are there any areas where you need help or support? List these areas and actively reach out to the existing help systems available to you.

▶ **Utilize Help Systems:** What are the existing help systems available? Research and make use of these resources to get the assistance you need.

▶ **Avoid Mistakes:** What intentional efforts will you make to avoid past mistakes? List these efforts and implement them to prevent future errors.

▶ **Celebrate Wins:** What wins do you need to celebrate or journalize? Identify your recent victories and take time to celebrate and document them for future inspiration.

▶ **Fail Forward:** How can you fail forward? Reflect on your failures and develop a strategy to turn setbacks into stepping stones for future success.

CHAPTER 8

My Story: Trusting God's Timing

CHAPTER HIGHLIGHTS

- God still answers prayers.
- Your waiting is part of your life adventure.
- Delay is neither refusal nor denial.
- In waiting, identify those that have gone through similar experiences, learn from them and when you identify someone in a similar waiting situation, encourage them.
- Could God be waiting on you, whilst you are waiting on God? Act on what God is waiting on you for.

THE GOD FACTOR

This can be regarded as the force majeure, the act of God, predetermination, or the sovereignty of God. The Sovereignty of God can be explained away as 'supreme power and authority,' 'superior independence'. God's sovereignty is God in control. When you pray, you are inviting God's sovereignty into that situation, you are submitting your inadequacies to God. The Bible teaches that God is sovereign, that He rules over all things.

All the people of the earth are regarded as nothing. He does as he pleases with the powers of heaven and the people of the earth. No one can hold back his hand or say to him: 'What have you done?'

Daniel 4: 35

God is present in all phases of your life, He is there in all seasons of your life, even when you feel He is not there. He is right amid every situation and circumstances, watching over you. God is with you – yesterday, today, and even till the end.

...And surely, I am with you always, to the very end of the age.

Matthew 28:2

In your story, God is the glory and the lifter of your head. If it had not been the Lord on my side and yours, you would have been consumed. The Bible says:

> *...because no one succeeds by strength alone.*
>
> **1 Samuel 2:9b**

You will be intrigued that some labour more than you, but God has counted you worthy to be a beneficiary of His blessings. It is therefore important to recognize the God factor in your success stories.

> *Unless the LORD builds the house, they labour in vain who build it; unless the LORD guards the city, the watchman stays awake in vain. It is vain for you to rise early, to sit up late, to eat the bread of sorrows; for so He gives His beloved sleep.*
>
> **Psalm 127: 1-2**

This can be seen in the lives of several individuals in the bible and in our times.

> *But by the grace of God, I am what I am, and His grace toward me was not in vain; but I*

laboured more abundantly than they all, yet not I, but the grace of God which was with me.

The apostle Paul says:

I have become as a wonder to many, but You are my strong refuge.

1 Corinthians 15:10

King David mentioned in Psalms:

My success — at which so many stand amazed — is because you are my mighty protector.

Psalm 71:7 (LBV)

If there is a God, then why does He allow pain and evil and why is he not helping everyone.

WHY DOES GOD ALLOW PAIN?

Often in everyday life, especially during the COVID–19 pandemic, when I speak to people about the good news of Jesus, I have encountered several questions: Why does God allow evil? Why does God allow wars and famine? Why do people suffer from cancer?

Why do people go through so much pain? What is the reason behind the loss of loved ones or loss of jobs? Is God evil? So many 'whys.' All these questions are valid, and I will try to address some and some I may not have answers to. When I eventually meet God face to face, I anticipate posing a few questions as well. One of the questions I can answer, certainly, is that God is not evil, He is a good God, a good father, a reliable friend, and a dependable and faithful companion. However, the question lingers: If He is good, why does He allow pain and evil?

> *"God is not evil; He is a good God."*

I will start by asking a few questions – did Jesus suffer? Did evil befall Jesus? Yes! So, if God can allow His son, Jesus Christ, to experience pain, he can allow it to happen, but remember He is not the cause of it. However, in return, He can bring good results, blessings, victories, out of that pain.

The Bible says:

> *And we know that in all things God works for the good of those who love him, who have been called according to his purpose.*

Romans 8:28

So, even when the devil brings evil occurrences, God can turn it around for good. God was able to bring salvation out of the pains of Jesus Christ. He can, as well, bring beauty out of the ashes you are experiencing or will experience. I may not understand why some events happen and how they happen, but I know He is with you, and He loves you dearly.

...If God is for us, who can be against us?

Romans 8:31

At times, God allows pain when the hedge is broken, but even in such situations, at the mercies of God, God can turn things around for good.

He that diggeth a pit shall fall into it; and whoso breaketh an hedge, a serpent shall bite him.

Ecclesiastes 10:8

When the hedge is broken, the protection is removed, and the city, your life is prone to invasion. However, God is our protection. God protects His people in different ways; by angels (Psalm 91:11–12), by provision - Elijah was fed by ravens, Elijah was fed by the Widow of Zarephath (1 Kings 17:2-16), by fire (2 Kings 1:9–10), by floods (Judges 5:21), through escape routes (Acts 9:24–25), by royal decrees (Ezra 6:11–12), and insomnia (Esther 6).

God's ways of protecting us are infinite.

In Job, chapters 1-3, God protected Job. Job suffered many trials and challenges from Satan, but God created boundaries that Satan could not cross and later, in Job, chapter 29, he overcame and excelled in all his projects and undertakings with restoration. God wants the best for you, He wants you happy, well and in His plan. No matter the pain you may be going through at this time, come to Jesus Christ and enjoy your benefits and promises in Christ Jesus.

God allows pain because He is going to be with you, God does not cause pain. He will strengthen you and help you.

> *He says: So, do not fear, for I am with you; do not be dismayed, for I am your God. I will strengthen you and help you; I will uphold you with my righteous right hand.*
>
> ***Isaiah 41:10***

"God allows pain because He is going to be with you, God does not cause pain."

If God is with me, why does it seem like He does not answer my prayers? Does God answer prayers? Let us delve into the next section to explore whether God answers prayers or not.

DOES GOD ANSWER PRAYERS?

Yes! God hears and answers prayers. At times, it may seem like the answers are delayed or prayers are not answered, leading to moments of doubt and some attempt to help God. Some individuals, in response, lose faith and take a position to declare that 'God is dead,' 'God does not exist', 'God does not answer prayers', 'It is sheer luck when prayers are answered'. However, all these are not valid positions.

I am confident that God answers prayers, and He is in the business of answering prayers. I have seen various instances recorded in the Bible, from friends, families, and even myself where God answered prayers. There are diverse examples of answers to prayers in the bible, I will share a few:

- Abraham's prayer for a child was answered based on God's promise - *Genesis 15:2-3; Genesis 21:1-8*.
- Jacob's prayer for a blessing answered based on God's promise - *Genesis 28:20-22; Genesis 32:9-12*.
- Hannah's prayer for a child - *1 Samuel 1:10-11, 19-20*.
- The Israelite prayers and cries for freedom - *Exodus 3:7-10*.
- Peter's prayer for release from the prison - *Acts 12:1-11*.
- My prayers – God has answered my prayers in

countless ways, to mention a few: authoring this book, protecting, providing, peace, getting married, giving birth to my children, my business, my career, and journey mercies.

Some reasons, why it may appear God does not answer prayers are:

▶ **Our timing and God's timing are different:** 2 Peter 3:8–9 reads: But do not forget this one thing, dear friends: With the Lord, a day is like a thousand years, and a thousand years are like a day. The Lord is not slow in keeping his promise, as some understand slowness. He is patient with you, not wanting anyone to perish, but everyone to come to repentance. You may desire answers to your prayers today and God may answer tomorrow, that is His choice.

He has made everything beautiful in its time...

Ecclesiastes 3:11 says:

▶ **Sin:** Doing terrible things never earns you good things. Sin is a deterrent that will always separate you from God.

God yearns to answer prayers, it is His desire, but sin separates.

> *Behold, the LORD's hand is not shortened, that it cannot save; neither is His ears heavy that it cannot hear: But your iniquities have separated you and your God, and your sins have hid his face from you, that he will not hear. For your hands are defiled with blood, and your fingers with iniquity; your lips have spoken lies, your tongue hath muttered perverseness.*

Isaiah 59:1–3

God hates sin and this may inhibit our relationship with God, leading to an unhealthy relationship with Him and hindering answers to prayers. You need to confess and get rid of anything that will come between you and God.

> *If I had cherished iniquity in my heart, the Lord would not have listened.*

Psalm 66:18

Sin can deter the answers to prayers. In the bible, Nehemiah had to confess a sin he did not commit to get answers to his prayers on behalf of the land of Israel. He said: I confess that we have sinned against you.

> *Yes, even my own family and I have sinned! We have sinned terribly by not obeying the commands, decrees, and regulations that you gave us.*

Nehemiah 1:6-7

You can hide things from people, but can you hide things from God? No! He sees all things. He knows all things.

▶ As parents, do you give your children everything they want? If an eight-years-old child requests a power car such as Ferrari, would you give the child that car? Without a doubt, you would wait for the child to be of age before you can consider buying the child a car. To start with, you may not even buy a Ferrari, subsequently, you may give a Ferrari. So, all this is because God loves you and He would not give you what will kill you. **God loves you and wants you to mature before He can give you some of the things you desire.**

... as long as an heir is underage, he is no different from a slave, although he owns the whole estate.

The bible says in Galatians 4:1

There is no place for underage and immaturity in ownership.

▶ **God grows your faith, matures you and your trust in Him, the same way a parent teaches a child to trust.**

If you... know how to give good gifts to your children, how much more will your heavenly Father give... to those who ask him.

Luke 11:13

▶ Children ask and trust parents to grant their requests, same as God, our father, expects us to identify a need, ask and trust that He will meet the need. Not trusting the process can appear that God does not answer prayers. This reminds me of an experience I had when I was newly married. I never asked for help and just assumed my husband should help. Quickly did I realise that I needed to ask; and when I started asking for help, I got help. Never assume, ask God, try asking God the big, trivial things and boom! The answers are trickling in at God's own time. God knows you need those things, but **He wants you to ask and trust.**

▶ **God will supply all your needs and not all your wants.**

But my God shall supply all your needs according to his riches in glory by Christ Jesus. A need is different from a want. God can ascertain a need from a want.

Philippians 4:19

Chapter 8

▶ **At times you expect answers to your prayers to be in a predefined way, but God can choose to answer in an unusual way.** A good example is praying to God for money and God, being the source of your wealth, can choose a creative way to provide the money. In your mind, you are stuck on only one source, that the funds will only be provided through your job. But God is creative and bent to provide through a different means – a rebate, refund, tax return, or an inheritance. Remember, God is your source. God says emphatically,

For every beast of the forest is mine, the cattle on a thousand hills. I know every bird of the mountains, and everything that moves in the field is mine. If I were hungry, I would not tell you, for the world is mine, and all it contains.

Psalm 50:10-12

▶ **Praying amiss can** hinder answers to prayers. This means praying wrongly and trying to convince or manipulate God to answer your prayers against His word, His principle, His law, and His character. It is not in God's character to lie, He will not because of your request change His character and lie, hence you may say He does not answer prayers.

When you ask, you do not receive, because you ask with wrong motives, that you may spend what you get on your pleasures.

James 4:3

▶ The King James version of the bible is even clearer – "Ye ask, and receive not, because ye ask amiss, that ye may consume it upon your lusts." For instance, you meet a handsome man, who is married and has children, and you ask God to make the man divorce his wife and become your husband, or the wife and children should die, so that you can become the wife. No! God will not answer such prayers, He is not a wicked God. You may feel this is a bit of an extreme situation, so, let me give you another scenario. I have in the past desired a job role. I prayed for it and felt disappointed when I did not get the job. I found out later that the organisation made a lot of people redundant a few weeks down the line. God knows the best and works all things for your good. In praying, I have heard people talk about praying God's will, yet they do not know what God's will is. God's will is God's word and God's word is expressed in the bible.

> *"At times you expect answers to your prayers to be in a predefined way and God can choose to answer in a different way."*

Never doubt it, God answers prayers, though answers to prayers may be delayed, called the waiting period. He uses prayers to align you with His purpose for your life. When you pray, be specific, and when He answers, you are rest assured that He answers prayers. When you pray, pray according to God's word, the bible, pray according to God's character: He is faithful, dependable, wonderful, powerful, all sufficient, and good. When you pray, remind Him of His promises. Nehemiah prayed to the Lord, saying:

Please remember what you told your servant Moses.

Nehemiah 1:8

You can imagine asking God to "remember." Yes. Nehemiah reminded God of a promise made to the land of Israel. You can remind God of His promises concerning your country, family, life, health, finances, business, career, and children. Does God forget? No! He does not forget. Did you have to remind God? No! But this helps you and reminds you to stand on the promises of God and receive the fulfilment of those promises. He answers prayers, keep praying, keep asking. Though it tarries or delays, wait for answers.

Does this imply there can be delay to what you ask God in prayer? What causes the delay in answers to your prayers? This will be explored in the next section.

WAITING: WHY ANSWERS TO PRAYERS ARE DELAYED

God answers prayers, however, prayers can be delayed. In times like this, everyone dislikes waiting - waiting in the traffic, waiting in the queue, waiting for a proposal answer, or waiting for results. You want answers quickly and sharply. The world system is built around everything happening quickly — Quick answers, fast results. God has made it clear that there is a season for everything, a season to be born, die, rejoice, and mourn. There is also a season of waiting.

I trust the Lord God to save me, and I will wait for him to answer my prayer.

Micah 7:7

After praying and asking, you want answers, and you may ask questions like – When Lord? How long do I have to wait? When will this happen? The period between the prayers and answers is the waiting period. When you sew you wait before harvest.

> *"Never doubt it, God answers prayers, though answers to prayers may be delayed, called the waiting period."*

Chapter 8

During this delay or waiting period, you may feel nothing is happening, but God has it all in perspective. Everyone waits, just that the phase of waiting differs for individuals. Let me give you few instances, in the bible and about myself, where there were waiting for answers to prayers:

▶ The Syrophoenician woman's prayer was answered, however not a word for a long time

Mark 7:26-29

▶ Paul sought the Lord thrice that "the thorn in the flesh" might be taken away from him, and he received no assurance that it should be taken away, but rather a promise that God's grace would be sufficient for him.

2 Corinthians 12

▶ I have waited for answers to some of my prayers and still waiting for a few.

So why would God delay answers to your prayers?

▶ **God is not in a hurry.** He is ageless and timeless. He is everlasting and He is eternal. He took a long time before sending Jesus to save the world. He is taking His time for the second coming. Remember that God is never in a hurry, but He is always on time.

▶ **God is allowing you to wait to build trust in Him.** Waiting is part of life and to get on well in the journey, you had better learn early and fast to trust God in the process.

▶ **God makes all things happen at His own time**.

He has made everything beautiful in its time. He has also set eternity in the human heart; yet no one can fathom what God has done from beginning to end.

Ecclesiastes 3:11

No one who waits for my help will be disappointed. If He said it, He would do it.

Isaiah 49:23

▶ Delay they say is not denial, your **delay is not a refusal.** The good news is God did not say 'no.' He may just be saying 'not yet.'

▶ A waiter serves in the restaurant. As you wait, are you serving, maybe serving in the church? **Serve others.** What you make happen to others will happen to you.

▶ **Do you believe?** Believing is faith. Do you have faith that God will answer your prayers or that your prayers have been answered? Faith is more than believing, it is beyond dreaming, thinking, or talking. **Faith is action.** Faith involves work, movement, activity, and stepping out. Faith is doing.

If people say they have faith, but do nothing, their faith is worth nothing.

James 2:14

What are the steps you need to take to see answers to your prayers?

.... faith without works is dead also.

James 2:26

What are you doing towards the manifesting of the answers to your prayers?

▶ **Are you expectant?** Are you expecting God to answer your prayers? Are you preparing for the answers to the prayers? Are you planning and putting things in place? When you make a financial investment, you expect a return. You work out the return on investment (ROI) even before the investment and plan for the ROI.

I wait expectantly, trusting God to help, for he has promised.

Psalm 130:5

▶ Lack of humility:

Relax, Daniel, he continued, 'do not be afraid. From the moment you decided to humble yourself to receive understanding, your prayer was heard, ...

Daniel 10: 12

▶ Prayers can be delayed by spiritual forces, this can be seen in the bible in Daniel 10: 12 -14, where the prince of Persia waylaid the answer to the prayer that was heard. Especially, verse 13, says: But I was waylaid by the angel- prince of the kingdom of Persia.

> *"Are you waiting on God? Or is God waiting on you?"*

Despite waiting for God to answer prayers, in some instances, God is waiting on you. Yes! God is waiting on you. Are you waiting on God? Or is God waiting on you? God may be waiting on you to obey a particular instruction, to mature spiritually, and be ready for the answers to the prayers.

Do not try to get out of anything prematurely. Let it do its work, so you become mature and well-developed.

James 1:4

In all, are you agitated concerning your waiting period: getting your marital partner, getting help, delivering your baby, healing, job opportunity, contract or job offer, solving a financial problem, repairing your credit history, buying your home, etc. Whatever it is, I want you to ponder on the above points to strengthen you and gain more insights.

> *For the vision is yet for an appointed time and it hastens to the end [fulfilment]; it will not deceive or disappoint. Though it tarries, wait [earnestly] for it, because it will surely come; it will not be behind hand on its appointed day.*
>
> **Habakkuk 2:3**
>
> *I am the Lord, and when it is time, I will make these things happen quickly.*
>
> **Isaiah 60:22**

Thanksgiving provides an answer to the situation faster. You may pray amiss but can never give thanks amiss.

In some instances, your story does not only feel like answers to the prayers are delayed. You feel God is silent, the silence is deafening, and the wait is unbearable. You feel that in your story, God is so far away. You do not even know how to pray about the issue anymore. The next section will explore this aspect of your story.

WHEN IT ALL DOES NOT SEEM TO MAKE SENSE

Sometimes you feel God is silent, the silence is deafening and so far, away. Let me tell you a story. Jesus was silent for a long time when an angry mob wanted to stone a woman caught in the act of adultery. It is wise to be silent when people are only interested in hearing a particular opinion or when they are so furious or full of strong emotions. Jesus remained silent for a long time until the angry mob ran out of their fury, emotions, and personal opinions, and then he gave them an audience. Another story is that of Job. God appeared silent, and he asked God numerous questions, and he kept asking God several questions.

At times, we have deep questions in our hearts, especially when it seems like God is so far away, and everything doesn't seem to make sense. When you are in pain and all doesn't add up, life seems hopeless, and it seems God is a million miles away and nowhere to be found. **God is watching over you, He is with you. Instead of stirring, God enters your pain and holds your hands. He gets down into it with you.** I remember the loss of my dad, God was with me, giving me warm, cosy hugs. He gave me peace on all sides. When my heart was too weak to pray, His shoulders were wide enough for me to rest on.

Chapter 8

The LORD is close to the broken-hearted and saves those who are crushed in spirit. I once heard a song - Lord, You Seem So Far Away, by a Christian artist, Don Moen.

Psalm 34:18

I WILL SING

Song by Don Moen:
Lord, you seem so far away.
A million miles or more,
  It feels today.
And though I haven't lost my faith,
I must confess right now,
  That it's hard for me to pray.

But I don't know what to say
And I don't know where to start.
But as you give the grace,
With all that's in my heart, I will sing,
  I will praise.

Even in my darkest time.
Through the sorrow and the pain.
I will sing,
I will praise.

Lift my hands to honor you,
Because your word is true. I will sing.
Lord, it is hard for me to see,
All the thought and plans you have for me.
But I will put my trust in you.
Knowing that you died to set me free (oh

thank God you died).
But I don't know what to say (what to say)
And I don't know where to start (where to start).
But as you give the grace,
With all that's in my heart, I will sing,
I will praise.

Even in my darkest time.
Through the sorrow and the pain, I will sing,
I will praise.
Lift my hands to honor you,
Because your word is true,
(say it again), I will sing
(Lord we sing to you),
I will praise.
Even in my darkest time.
Through the sorrow and the pain, I will sing,

I will praise.
Lift my hands to honor you,
Because your word is true. I will sing,
I will sing, I will sing.

Oh, we sing to the Lord tonight, Hallelujah.
We sing to you Lord. Oh, we lift our voices
And worship you.

We sing to the Lord,
We sing, we sing, we sing We sing, we sing.

Oh, we worship you Lord.
Oh, thank you. Lord
I will sing.

(Oh, yes, sing)

I will sing (Jesus).

No matter how you feel or how unclear the situation may seem, you can trust that God is with you. He has the power to transform all your setbacks into a remarkable comeback. As you navigate through these challenges, you have the opportunity to share your story in the various styles mentioned earlier. Whether it's through writing, speaking, or another form of expression, your story has the potential to inspire and encourage others, showcasing the resilience and hope that comes from trusting in God's plan.

What is impossible with man is possible with God.

Jesus says in Luke 18:27

Are you burdened with doubt, anger, pain, fear, frustration, grief, confusion, or unanswered questions? It's natural to feel overwhelmed by these emotions, but you don't have to carry them alone. Cast all your cares upon God, for He is ready to listen and provide comfort. Open your heart to Him and share every fear, worry, and question you have. Trust in His infinite wisdom and love to guide you through even the darkest times. By entrusting your burdens to God, you can find peace and clarity amid the chaos.

Chapter 8

If you are tired from carrying heavy burdens, come to me and I will give you rest.

Matthew 11:28

> *God is watching over you, He is with you. Instead of stirring, God enters your pain and holds your hands. He gets down into it with you.*

When words fail you, you can sing or praise God, worshiping and adoring Him. He is always with you, He is for you, and He can handle all your questions, fears, doubts, and concerns. As you present your case before God, feel free to lament if you need to, expressing yourself openly and honestly. Trust in Him, for He is able to do new and wonderful things in your life. Through worship and praise, you can find comfort and reassurance, knowing that God is listening and will provide for you in His perfect timing.

Behold, I will do a new thing; now shall it spring forth; shall ye not know it? I will even make a way in the wilderness, and rivers in the desert.

The Bible says in Isaiah 43:19

You need to focus, have faith, believe, and obey God and He will come through for you.

CALL TO ACTION

▶ **Identify Your Pain Points:** Reflect on specific challenges or difficulties you are facing right now.

▶ **Seek Help and Support:** Look for available resources, support groups, or individuals who can help.

▶ **Connect with Others:** Reach out to fellow believers or Christians who may have experienced similar struggles.

▶ **Evaluate Your Waiting Period:** Consider what you are waiting on God for and if there are steps you should take in the meantime.

▶ **Follow Divine Instructions:** Identify and act upon any instructions you believe God has given you.

▶ **Reflect on Lessons Learned:** Think about the insights and lessons you have gained during your waiting period.

▶ **Apply Lessons to Future Situations:** Use the lessons learned to prepare for and navigate future waiting periods more effectively.

▶ **Encourage Others:** Identify someone currently in a waiting period and find ways to support and encourage them.

CHAPTER 9

My Story: Wins And Pains

CHAPTER HIGHLIGHTS

- Life has different phases and seasons.
- Identify and act on trade-offs for progress.
- Recognize your potential to bless others.
- Painful experiences can lead to change.
- Do not abuse the privilege of access to others.
- Setting boundaries is acceptable.
- Keep learning and stay open to change.

MY WINS

In a previous chapter, I provided a brief overview of my life. In this chapter, I would like to delve into the details of some of my challenges and victories. They all sum up as my wins; some, I achieved on my own by the grace of God and some I achieved through help from others.

YOUR WINS

This may just be the way I am wired, when I see individuals succeed, I am genuinely happy for them. Hence your wins, others' wins. I have countless people that have given me joy and fulfilment, especially when I am an active participant in the process of actualizing the success. I believe their success is also my success. In fact, if caution is not exercised, you will think it is my win when I hear the victory news. It gives me immense pleasure to help and serve others. When I see a genuine need, my heart is drawn towards getting the need met. Your wins are mine. In mentoring, counselling, caring, and supporting others, I give recommendations and when I receive reports of overcoming challenges, there is a pleasure, joy, satisfaction, and fulfilment that comes with it. The same applies when I pray about an issue and there is a breakthrough, I celebrate, I rejoice. In some instances, when I coach individuals to get new jobs, purchase new properties, pray about issues, and see them happen, it gives me great joy.

SALVATION

This is the absolute best decision that I have ever made. I was once a miserable young girl, full of worries and cares of this world until I met a lady on my first day at the university. She was caring and kind to me, and I liked her; her kindness was unusual and that caught my attention. Theodore Roosevelt said, "People don't care how much you know until they know how much you care." Her love was genuine and palpable, and she helped me to settle into campus life. I was ready to explore life in ignorance, but through her genuine love, I met with Jesus Christ. I accepted to attempt her lifestyle, knowing that was what gave her such joy, peace, and love. You may want to attempt that love if you don't have it yet. It is accepting to open your heart and making the decision to have a relationship with Jesus Christ, asking Him to forgive you all your wrong doings and help you start a relationship with Him.

A huge shout-out to the faithful people of God Jesus Christ used doggedly to establish me in faith. I may not have found this thrilling relationship without their gritty love and opportunity to grow. This I will encourage you to do, be determined to establish a soul in Christ. Mentor someone, establish someone in faith to keep the faith.

How beautiful the experience will be when you get to heaven, and someone made heaven just because of your sacrifices.

The decision to accept the love of Jesus Christ was a great detour in my journey—a detour for the best. The decision came with several prices (sacrifices) and prizes (rewards); it has been extremely rewarding. Are you discouraged, tired, frustrated, and hopeless, come to Jesus Christ just the way you are. This decision is not about a religion, what to do and what not to do. It is about you, enjoying peace in this world that is full of heartaches, pains, evils, and betrayals.

> *"No one cares how much you know, until they know how much you care."*
>
> ***Theodore Roosevelt***

CAREER

For my first degree, I bagged a Bachelor of Science (B.Sc.) Honours in International Relations from the prestigious university of Obafemi Awolowo University, Osun state, then I proceeded to Lagos state, also in Nigeria, for my Master in Business Administration (MBA). I got my Master of Science (M.Sc.) in Information Systems from the University of Liverpool, UK; along with several Information Systems

Certifications – Oracle OCDBA, Business Analysis, Project Management – Prince2, Agile, Amazon Web Services (AWS), Google Cloud, Microsoft Azure, Information Technology Infrastructure Library (ITIL), SCRUM, Six Belt etc. All these, I achieved by the grace and mercies of God. These professional qualifications and training were acquired with a price. They are part of my success stories. Studying, writing exams, and passing all the steps at divergent phases are all wins for me. All these feats have helped in my attainment of several wins, working as a consultant in several organisations and institutions, and meeting several individuals of diverse ethnics and origins. The exposure hugely formed who I am today. I would never take this for granted, working with diverse professionals with multi- diverse ethnic groups and cultures.

At this point, I would like to mention some acts of God in my career path. I believe they are miracles of God; I believe in miracles. Just a quick perspective: when you graduate in my country of origin, Nigeria, you must have some strong connection to get your Curriculum Vitae (CV) or resume through, to the right person or corridor of life, which is appalling. I knew I was good and wanted more from life and myself. I would walk the streets of Victoria Island in Lagos state, a location where various banks, Oil and Gas head-offices and human resource (HR) companies are situated. I distributed my CV to several head offices, facing obstacles even with the securities

Chapter 9

personnel, not to mention the secretaries—sigh! In desperation, all I could do was knock on heaven's door. The act of God, till today remains a mystery as to how my CV found its way to a bank, then called, 'First Atlantic' bank. Miraculously, I was shortlisted and thereafter interviewed, and I joined the banking industry. This act of God changed the trajectory of my life.

In my career, I must mention and acknowledge my line managers who have been amazing. From the days of T-Rock, Sukky, Jacs, DJ, Isi, the list is huge, however these ones have nicknames, hence I have mentioned them. The one that choked my life, I am in fact incredibly grateful to, as it pushed me to explore new terrains. You can see that in all these are victories. Victories of over two decades of work experience. I am grateful! You may see it as luck or coincidence; someone once told me that it is because I am a lovely person. But definitely, this is more than coincidence or luck because I have encountered lovely people that never experienced pleasant line managers or colleagues. As such, I see this as a victory, a miracle, an act of God. Many of my work colleagues, today, are my friends and acquaintances.

RELOCATION

The start of a career in the banking industry made me comfortable, and loyal to my country. Then I focused on building my family, with unwavering support from my immediate family. I was equipped with assistance, a chauffeur, and childcare support. Life was good in my country, it was a hospitable, warm, fun-loving, and cultured atmosphere, particularly in the millennium. So, the idea of relocating held little appeal, especially to an unfamiliar climatic colder environment. I never wanted to relocate, not at all. However, circumstances led me to make a challenging decision—one of the toughest I have faced—to start afresh. As I mentioned earlier, I eventually agreed to relocate. My parents encouraged me to stand by and support my husband, making the decision all the more difficult. But interestingly, I am loving it now. As the saying goes, home is indeed where the heart is. Reflecting on this journey, I am reminded of ***1 Corinthians 1:30:***

> *Everything that we have—right thinking and right living, a clean slate, and a fresh start—comes from God by way of Jesus Christ.*

Chapter 9

RELOCATING TO THE UK

There were loads of cultural shocks when I arrived in the United Kingdom, the cold weather, the pet experience, the 'mind your business' attitude, the absence of friends and families, doing all the chores independently, public transport, waiting at the bus-stop, catching the train, converting my native currency to pounds sterling, pushing the buggy, the daunting job hunt, and the challenge of lacking the UK experience, phew! I almost ran back. It was just too much for me. The fact that I did not hastily retreat remains a significant personal triumph for me.

Are you considering a fresh start in any area of your life? Why not give it a go? A fresh start can be refreshing. You can do it—I did! By the grace and help of God. I learnt and I am still adapting to a new culture, making new friends, and expanding my social circle. I am even rediscovering a few things here and there. I am grateful to God for the tenacity, the privilege, and the exposure.

RELOCATING WITHIN UK

This came with its own challenges: admitting the children into new schools, childcare challenges, knowing no one in the area, and having to start all over again. Despite the challenges, God has settled me and my entire household and made the land, our Goshen, a place of plenty and comfort.

This was a trade-off for me, a decision made after undergoing a previous relocation and then opting for it again. Through these experiences, I have learnt and realised that **you have to give- up to grow-up.** In life, I have had a few trade-offs, realising that surrendering some valued aspects is often necessary to actualize your full potential. You must learn to see trade-offs as opportunities to grow, expand and develop. Trade-offs compel you to make difficult personal changes, which ordinarily you would not consider. Change is personal, achievable, and rewarding. Although, some of these adjustments were not worth it, while some were, for example: relocating was worth it, as it led to personal changes and thereafter personal growth. Life will bring several trade-offs; you need to identify the ones with opportunity and grab them and avoid the ones that are not worth it. Most successful people identify a good trade-off and do a lot of them, whilst the unsuccessful ones make bad trade-offs. You need to take advantage of the moment and when God is leading you, obey. Obey! Obedience is better than sacrifice and delayed obedience is disobedience. Trade- offs are also known as deals, in some instances. Good deals do not stay around for long, harness it quickly.

> *"You have to give-up to grow-up."*

Chapter 9

MY PAINS: MY GRIEFS

Undoubtedly, no one wants to experience grief, yet it is an inevitable part of life that we will experience at some point. I have had some losses, particularly two major losses. The loss of my grandmother and my dad. My dad's loss was more painful as it was unexpected and regrettably, I did not get the chance to bid him a proper goodbye. It was a shock I did not envisage. Without a doubt, this was a very painful and emotional period of my life. It has been one of my darkest nights. However, I emerged from it with the realisation that it is alright to grieve. I appreciate everyone that stood by me in this phase. A big shout-out to everyone that reached out with warm hugs, visits, messages, and flowers from all around the world. The church of God and most especially the Holy Spirit were of great comfort, just as said in God's word:

> *Blessed are those who mourn, for they will be comforted.*
>
> **Matthew 5:4.**

In the journey of grief, acceptance plays a pivotal role. It's crucial to understand that acceptance doesn't diminish the pain or make it any less excruciating. Denying the grief can complicate the healing process. Acceptance, in this context, involves recognizing and embracing the reality of the situation and appreciating that it cannot be altered. It's about acknowledging the pain and finding the strength to move forward within the confines of this new reality.

The sad news of those two losses and several others that I have experienced came with disbelief. In most instances, I would say in shock, "but I just spoke with him or her not too long ago"—a few minutes, hours, or even days ago. Such is life, the denial, the disbelief. I vividly remember entering the morgue, praying, and believing the dead would rise. At least, Jesus had raised Lazarus, and been redeemed by Jesus Christ, I had faith.

However, unfortunately, my dead loved ones did not arise. At that moment, I realised that this was for real. When you grieve, **acceptance is key**. Acceptance does not mean it does not hurt; it does not make it less painful. **Acceptance of grief** is the realisation and acceptance of reality and appreciating that you cannot change the situation. Rather, accepting and moving forward with your new reality. "God, grant me the serenity to accept the things I cannot change, the courage to change the things I can, and the wisdom to know the difference." — Reinhold Niebuhr. If at any time you struggle to accept grief, as individuals respond differently to an emotional experience, especially grief, you may want to reach out for support. The section in this book, on how to identify pain and resolve the pain points will be of help.

It is important to realise that the devil, most times,

plays a guilt game on individuals grieving the death of a loved one. You must take ownership and not let the devil leave you in resentment and bitterness. Take an approach to make peace with yourself, by surrendering your pain and helplessness to Jesus Christ. He is indeed a true succour, present help in times of need. When you surrender to God, you are inviting Him to take over. No matter the season of your life – the good, the bad, God can work all things for your good.

We know that in all things God works for the good of those who love him.

Romans 8:28

I have experienced, personally, my share of grief, let me discuss a few points on how God used it to foster my growth.

You will wonder, can anything positive emerge from grief? Can any good come from a deep loss aside from a heavy heartache? No one can appreciate water like a thirsty person. No one can appreciate food like a starving person. Similarly, no one can appreciate comfort like someone who is grieving. Additionally, I will explore how grief can have negative impacts. As the loss of a loved one, your life is intertwined with can be exhausting and life changing.

Acceptance of grief is key.

POSITIVES OF GRIEF

▶ **Experience the Holy Spirit's comfort**: You never know God can heal until you get a disease, and He heals you. You never know God can provide until you have a need. I heard, read, and knew the Holy Spirit comforts. However, it was a first-hand experience to benefit from the Holy Spirit's comfort at a grieving period of my life. The bible says in Matthew 5:4: *Blessed are those who mourn, for they shall be comforted.* I experienced the comfort of the Holy Spirit through God's spirit, His word (bible), gospel music and God's people. When you are in grief, remember Jesus Christ promised you the comfort of the Holy Spirit. He is such a good father, faithful and right there, ready to help and comfort you on all sides. He always has your best interest at heart.

▶ **The realisation that God is with me**: I literally felt and experienced God's love, warm embrace, and breath- taking hugs. This was so real; words cannot explain the experience.

When you go through deep waters, I will be with you. When you go through rivers of difficulty, you will not drown. When you walk through the fire of oppression, you will not be burned up; the flames will not consume you.

Isaiah 43:2

Chapter 9

No matter how tough the times and the pains, it will not consume you. No! The storms of life or tough times may appear shattering, but it will not shatter or wreck you. Irrespective of how you feel about God today, you can be rest assured that God is with you. He is a present help in times of need. He is right with you. He was with me in my most daunting period, the grief periods, He is still with me and will always be with you too. Are you full of pain, doubt, anger, fear, grief, frustration, confusion, or queries? Take it all to God. He is with you, he is for you, and he can manage all your pains, grief, questions, and concerns. The Bible says:

... If God is for us, who can be against us?

Romans 8:31

▶ **God used grief to get my attention:** C. S. Lewis wrote, "God whispers to us in our pleasures, speaks in our conscience, but shouts in our pain." Pain is God's megaphone to reach out to us. We rarely change when we see the light, but we change when we feel the heat.

Sometimes it takes a painful experience to make us change our ways.

Proverbs 20:30

▶ **God got me looking ahead to eternity:** My experience interestingly got me looking towards eternity, more, bearing in mind that I will see my loved one again. In 1 Thessalonians 4:13, the bible says: We do not want you to be ignorant about those who have died. We do not want you to grieve like other people who have no hope. It is reassuring that those who die in Christ are only sleeping in the Lord and you, and I will see them again.

I have imagined several times, what the reunion in heaven would be like, meeting several saints and characters in the bible – Paul, Timothy, John the Baptist, Enoch, Deborah, Ruth, Esther, Mary, etc, I imagine getting to heaven and seeing my dad, grandmother, and all loved ones that has passed onto glory. The Bible says:

These little troubles are getting us ready for an eternal glory that will make all our troubles seem like nothing. Things that are seen do not last forever, but things that are not seen are eternal. This is why we keep our minds on the things that cannot be seen.

2 Corinthians 4:17-18

Have you ever pondered on why God did not take you home immediately you accepted and gave your life to Jesus Christ? He chose to leave you here to grow your character. Your car, career, clothes, jewelleries, and houses would not go with you to eternity; however, your character will. As such, all the pains and troubles you have gone through and still going through is building your character, preparing you for eternity. My pain surely did grow me.

"God whispers to us in our pleasures, speaks in our conscience, but shouts in our pain."

C. S. Lewis

▶ **God brings out good in every situation:** As much as God does not do evil, He has the ability to bring good out of every situation. You can decide to make the pain embitter or empower you. I am sure you will prefer to make your pain empower you, I chose to make the experience make me better and not bitter.

▶ **Appreciation of life:** Loss helps you appreciate the value of life. Many times when your alarm buzzes, you may hit the snooze button, casually attributing your awakening to the alarm. In reality, the alarm can only wake you up because you still have life, the breath in you. The handheld phone alarm which used to wake my dad, cannot wake him up anymore.

▶ **Grateful for everyday:** Everyday here on earth is a privilege. You are alive today by the grace and mercies of God. Some younger, older people and even age-mates are dead today. In other words, that you are alive today, you need to be grateful and not take it for granted.

"Yesterday is history, tomorrow is a mystery, today is a gift of God, which is why we call it the present."

Bill Keane

▶ **Make every moment count:** The loss of my loved ones made me appreciate and treasure every moment spent with them; the memories were all that is left. As such, you want to make every moment count; the moments are the memories that lives on after the loss of a loved one. I think back on the fond memories of times spent with my loved ones, making them happy, and I found joy, and happiness as I remembered those moments I had with them.

"In seeking happiness for others, you will find it in yourself."

Unknown

▶ **Identification of what is important in life:** Life is simple; however, life has been complicated.

"Life is really simple, but we insist on making it complicated."
Confucius

The grief experiences made me realise the particularly important things in life and focus less on the trivial things. One of the importance of these experiences is the legacy, like sharing my story and letting posterity benefit from my experiences.

▶ **More clarity on how I want to live:** It helped me to focus on how I want to live my life. With the understanding of what is important to me in life, I could clearly state how I want to live my life and what I want to do before I die, and the legacies I want to be known for. It made it clearer on how I did not want to live my life.

NEGATIVES OF GRIEF: MISTAKES YOU WANT TO AVOID

▶ **Denial:** It is important you do not live in denial; the loss has happened and needs to be identified and accepted. This may be a hard nut to crack, but you need to crack it irrespective of how hard or long it takes. I was able to achieve this by the grace of God. That same grace is available, ask for help from the source – God.

▶ **Guilt play:** The devil has a way of making you feel guilty, pondering on what you could have done better that could have avoided death. Never let the devil play a guilt game with your mind. Set yourself free from the guilt and battle of the mind. Joyce Meyer authored a book – The battlefield of the mind that details the battles that exist in our minds. You need to fight that battle and win in your mind.

▶ **You do not have to have an explanation:** With the loss of a loved one, most times you want to know, why? There is a feeling of wanting to know why? Why me? Why did it happen? Knowing why neither explains the loss nor lessens the pain. God has not promised us an explanation for everything that happens in the world. No! But He promised everyone that follows Jesus, that you are not going to go through any of it on your own. The Bible says:

When you go through deep waters, I will be with you. When you go through rivers of difficulty, you will not drown. When you walk through the fire of oppression, you will not be burned up; the flames will not consume you.

Isaiah 43:2

▶ **Why me? In moments of pain, many ask these questions:** Why me? When you are faced with adversity, grief, or pain, it can be a natural reaction to ask, "Why me?" You can feel pity for yourself and wallow in it. The questions asked can be from a victim mindset or perspective. You, sometimes, ask not because you want to know, but from a place of victimisation. It took me some time to journey from **Why me? to Why not me?** It was a deep experience, a journey of faith for me. I have had and still have a fair share of challenges and as clearly stated, in this life, you will have challenges. In grief, you can still see how God can be so good to you, so the question should be **why not you?** Hence, avoid the question, 'why me?' The bible says in James 1:2: *Count it all joy, my brothers, when you meet trials of various kinds.*

"God, grant me the serenity to accept the things I cannot change, the courage to change the things I can, and the wisdom to know the difference."

Reinhold Niebuhr

In the book of Job, in the first thirty-seven chapters, Job questioned, 'why': *"Why is this happening to me? Why are you allowing this? Why so much pain? Why so much discomfort? Why haven't you answered my prayers?"* In chapter 38, Job stops asking and God said: *I have some questions for you.*

- Job 38:3. Afterward, in subsequent two chapters, God erupts Job with questions that only God could answer. Job stopped questioning, and he started trusting. He replied to the Lord: *I know that you can do anything, and no one can stop you. You asked, 'Who is this that questions my wisdom with such ignorance?' It is I—and I was talking about things. I knew nothing about, things far too wonderful for me...I take back everything I said, and I sit in dust and ashes to show my repentance.* - Job 42:2-3, 6.

▶ **Embrace your challenges, accept your grief, and rely on God.**

▶ **Negative emotions:** The loss of a loved one can be overwhelming and can be life changing. You want to avoid the negative emotions such as shock, depression, insomnia, fear, anger, bitterness, guilt, resentment, anxiety, and emotional withdrawal. Most individuals experience shock initially, however conscious efforts and support should be taken to overcome these negative emotions. As much as some of these emotions are natural, never judge or compare yourself to others, as responses to grief differ in individuals. Remember your experience is unique. Treating yourself kindly can go a long way in supporting you till recovery.

▶ **Never get stuck:** It is alright to grieve but never get stuck in the grief process. If you need to weep, please weep. If you need to have an emotional outburst again, go ahead. Grief is not what you desire, I do not desire it, but when it occurs, you have the right to express your emotions. I chose to express my emotions. Rick Warren once said, "You do not get over a loss. You cannot go under it; you cannot go around it. You have got to go through the grief. And if you are scared to express emotion and refuse to go through it, that is where you get stuck."

▶ **Expressing grief in unhealthy ways:** You want to let out grief in healthy ways. Jesus never played out His grief in wrong or unhealthy ways. The Bible says Jesus was a man accustomed to sorrows. The Bible also says, when his friend, Lazarus died, Jesus grieved. He even wept! If Jesus wept, it is OK for you to weep, when needed. Let out the tears. Jesus Christ was expressive. Being expressive emotionally is not a weakness. However, there are two unhealthy reactions to loss: One is **repression**, and the other is **suppression**. Repression is when you unconsciously try to block painful thoughts from your mind. Suppression is when you do it consciously. You intentionally say, *"I am not going to think about that hurt. I am not going to think about that pain. I am going to put my head down and move* *forward."* Rick Warren. Not expressing your emotions when you grieve is an error, **it is dangerous.**

▶ **It can discourage you:** The loss of a loved one is discouraging and can be overwhelming. However, you do not want to stay in this state for too long. This can have side effects: depression, loneliness, low energy, loss of appetite, anxiety, even to the extent of denying the existence of God. See this state–the loss of a loved one– as a temporal state. Take your time to come through it and harness all the support available. Your lost loved one would not want you in this state for too long.

▶ **Unresolved grief:** This can be a complex grief; this can take longer than usual. It can be severe and intense for the individual. Unresolved grief happens when you live in denial of the current situation. In most instances, people may never know that the sufferer ever lost a loved one, for example, a miscarriage. As such, the support network may not identify this sufferer in order to provide the support required. The refusal to accept the loss of a loved one can lead to unresolved grief, which is better to avoid.

▶ **Traumatic grief:** This can happen when the loss of a loved one is traumatic, and you relive the memories as flashbacks. Whether it is an accident, suicide, or murder, the sufferer may feel like they are 'losing their mind. To avoid this negativity, seeking help is crucial. Cry, or lament if you need to, talk about it if it will help, and find coping mechanisms. Exercise can help to exert pent-up energy. While the memories are hurting, you do not want to deny or ignore them.

GOSSIP

Gossip can be referred to as a casual or unconstrained conversation or reports about an individual or other persons and it involves details that might be unkind, disapproving, and are not confirmed to be true. Gossip wrecks relationships, friendships, families, and churches.

A gossip betrays a confidence, but a trustworthy person keeps a secret.

Proverbs 11:13.

As an individual, do you betray the confidence of others or not? Ask yourself this question; that gist you told, was the person you shared it with a part of the problem or part of the solution to the situation? Gossip can make you feel important, current, or fun at the expense of another person. The Bible says:

Do not go about spreading slander among your people.

Leviticus 19:16.

You do not want the fury of God. Whoever slanders their neighbour in secret, I will put to silence.

Psalm 101:5.

This includes the listener and the speaker of the gossip. The Bible says the listener is wicked:

A wicked person listens to deceitful lips; a liar pays attention to a destructive tongue.

Proverbs 17:4

Gossip can also be an abuse of access. When you have access to an individual, you should count it as a privilege and exercise caution in sharing details or information about the individual. In the bible, David, Jeremiah, and Moses experienced gossip.

In Psalm 41, King David expressed the unpleasant result of gossip:

> *My enemies say of me in malice, 'When will he die, and his name perish?' When one of them comes to see me, he speaks falsely, while his heart gathers slander; then he goes out and spreads it around. All my enemies whisper together against me; they imagine the worst for me, saying, 'A vile disease has afflicted him; he will never get up from the place where he lies.' Even my close friend, someone I trusted, one who shared my bread, has turned against me.*
>
> **Psalm 41:5-9**

Jeremiah's messages were not accommodated. He said:

> *I hear many whisperings, 'Terror on every side! Denounce him! Let us denounce him!' All my friends are waiting for me to slip, saying, 'Perhaps he will be deceived; then we will prevail over him and take our revenge on him.'*
>
> **Jeremiah 20:10**

In Numbers 12, Moses had his own fair share of gossip. Moses had siblings named Miriam and Aaron who got caught up in gossiping about him. They began to talk against Moses because of his Cushite wife, for he had married a Cushite. God called all three of them to a meeting. When they all came out of their tents, He spoke to Miriam and Aaron, telling them that Moses was His prophet and that what they did was wrong. Immediately, God affected Miriam with leprosy because she was the originator of the gossip and she spoke to her younger brother, Aaron, to join her. You may wonder, and say that is terrible, but would you not wish for something to happen to those who gossip about you? But, anyway, you are not God. After God placed leprosy on Miriam, Aaron acknowledged their sin against Moses, and he asked Moses to pray for Miriam's healing. Then, Moses asked God to heal her. He prayed for the person who had spoken ill of him. And after seven days, God healed Miriam. If God detests gossip this bad, you can imagine how He hates it when people speak evil of others or gossip about others.

"Whoever slanders their neighbour in secret, I will put to silence."

Bible

Gossip may be ingrained into some societies, but it is better to treat others the way you want to be treated. You want to be intentional, not to gossip about others.

As an individual experiencing gossip stemming from abuse of access, it separated me from the individuals. The matter escalated and exaggerated, and I was hurt, hugely. I felt disappointment, and frustration, and was heartbroken. Especially, because it came from people, I least expected it from. It was refreshing to report the matter to God. So, tell
God all and He will fight the battles for you, even more than you can imagine.

I discovered that most of these gossips sprouted out of jealousy. And to make it juicy, because it had a baseless foundation, several unconfirmed details were added for exaggeration. I gained knowledge the hard way, never to give people the opportunity to have anything negative to say about you. When such gossip goes around and is not based or founded on anything substantial, the listeners will become your defender. God will raise a standard against rumour monger(s).

As draining and demoralising as the episodes can be, you must forgive and heal for your own peace. I was able to overcome mine by praying for the individuals. Pray for the grace to forgive and even forget. Now, if you ask me to summarise some episodes, I may not be able to relay the details. Though some stayed with me, honestly most, if not all, are forgotten.

My summation is, do not repay anyone evil for evil. Be careful to do what is right in the eyes of everyone. If it is possible, as far as it depends on you, live at peace with everyone. Do not take revenge, my dear friends, but leave room for God's wrath, for it is written: It is mine to avenge; I will repay, says the Lord. - Romans 12:17-19. When you hand-over a matter to God, God is a great avenger, He will fight and defend you better than you can do or imagine. He will exceed your imagination.

Chapter 9

BETRAYAL

I have had my fair share of betrayals as well. Kindly ask yourself these questions: Was Jesus Christ betrayed? Was Jesus Christ misunderstood? Did people gossip about Jesus Christ?

Yes! He went through all these pains. If Jesus went through all these and remains victorious, you should be encouraged. No matter who you are, God's purpose in your life is to make you more like Jesus, which is why you are called a Christian, Christ-like. To do that, God will take you through the same things Jesus went through. What joy it brings that Jesus Christ overcame, you will overcome. I overcame my fair share and even when this occurs again in the future, I know I will overcome, and you will too.

In some instances, I have helped individuals who backstabbed me. It was disappointing and very painful, especially when these help and support were sacrificial. At different instances, I wanted to stop assisting people, some, I wanted to run away from and avoid them like plagues. Those moments were draining as I felt used and dumped. At some point, I thought I could exonerate myself. However, the Holy Spirit is a good counsel, including God's word, and important people in my life. I had to forgive and let go. Forgiving is the right step to take in this situation, for they do not know what they are doing.

I must be honest, this can be exceedingly challenging, but possible by God's grace that is sufficient. But What Will Jesus Do (WWJD)—He will have compassion. He had compassion on them, because they were harassed and helpless... - Matthew 9:36. God forgives us. He is a God of several chances. No matter how frustrating, hurt, or betrayed you feel, Jesus will always respond with compassion. This is the grace you and I can explore.

However, trust is abused. So, in forgiving, you must let the individual(s) rebuild the trust that has been breached. Lack of trust in a relationship can never build a warm, comfortable relationship as God desires. Friendship, or any relationship without trust is awkward. When trust is lost in a relationship, a lot is lost. I once read, "Trust is the currency of any relationship. Once it's gone, the value diminishes."- Unknown. Also, Proverbs 20:6 says: *Many people claim to be loyal, but it is hard to find a trustworthy person.* However, with God's grace, trust can be rebuilt. In my own experience, I maintained peace with the individuals, taking on the lessons I learnt along with me in the relationship. I exercised vulnerability in some of the relationships, and some, indeed, rebuilt their trust and we now have a better relationship. While some are yet to convince me; in such instances, I have learnt to define the depth of the relationship, defining boundaries, yet being at peace with the individuals.

Chapter 9

During my first Christmas in the United Kingdom, I was to attend a Christmas service in winter, roughly three miles away from home. Well dressed, looking gorgeous in my high heels and native attire, I got to church. I left my jacket in the car, as the church was warm – well heated. After the service, I stepped out and realised that the car that brought me could not take me back. I had to walk back home in heels, with no jacket, in the very chilly winter weather. This was on one of the days when there was no public transportation on Christmas day. I wept my eyes out and got home with numb toes. Today, I have a better relationship with the person that disappointed me. Though the pain was excruciating that day, but, today, the rest is history. If I did not let go, I would not have let God.

In another instance, I decided to give out a loan, the individual stopped picking up my calls after a while. I did not realise this until I tried calling with another person's phone. Till today, the loan is a bad debt. I gave a loan to another person; it took several years to get the funds paid down. The good thing from both instances is that the individuals would never come back for another loan.

At some point, I wanted to hold off helping people, however, the bible says:

> *Let us not become weary in doing good, for at the proper time we will reap a harvest if we do not give up. Therefore, as we have opportunity,*

let us do good to all people, especially to those who belong to the family of believers. In not being tired of doing good.

Galatians 6: 9-10

I have helped several other individuals with loans, and they have paid back and shown gratitude. Remember, you are just a channel of God's blessings.

'I will bless you,' God says to Abraham, 'and you will be a blessing...and all people on earth will be blessed through you'.

Genesis 12:2-3

The principle of being blessed to be a blessing is reinforced all through the scriptures. Part of God's purpose for you includes being a blessing to other people. It is vital to reiterate that your purpose as a believer is to be a blessing.

> *"Your purpose as a believer is to be a blessing."*

The fact is that God has blessed you, and He desires for you to bless others as well. God wants to prosper you beyond meeting your needs, which is the bare minimum.

He does not want you to be a dam, but a river. Dam stinks, but a flowing river oozes freshness.

Being a blessing is like a channel, a river, flowing to others. Emphasis is on you being a blessing by giving rather than getting. Prosperity for purpose is God's desire for you. God wants you to abound in every good works.

> *"Forgive for your peace and keep blessing."*

Despite the pains, challenges, and victories in navigating my life, there were also nuggets and takeaways that proved helpful. Here are some key points I have highlighted.

TOP 15 NUGGETS

▶ **God uses your pain to help others:** This is redemptive pain, and it is the highest and best use of the pain you can go through. God does not want you to waste a hurt. He does not want you to waste your story.

> *[God] comforts us in all our troubles so that we can comfort others. When they are troubled, we will be able to give them the same comfort God has given us.*
>
> **2 Corinthians 1:4**

Today, I can share my grief experience because I have encountered the situation, and I can relate. As much as I may not understand how exactly it feels to experience the loss of your own loved ones, I can empathize because I have walked that path before.

▶ **Life is in phases and seasons; every season comes with challenges and wins.** Make effective use of every moment, make it count. "Every season in life has its purpose and lessons to teach; we must be willing to embrace them and grow." Enjoy, and celebrate when it is the season to rejoice. Mourn, grief, and lament when it is the season to grief. The Bible in Ecclesiastes, chapter 3, makes it clear that **there is a season and time for everything.** Whatever season of life you are in, today, make it count.

▶ **Trust God:** Rely completely on God, all the way. He is dependable and reliable. He can make a message out of your mess. My life is a report of how God can make somebody out of nobody. He is a good father; he can father you beyond your imagination. He is so close, He is with you always, till the end of time. Even if you think that situation will crush you, I have good news for you, when you rely on Jesus Christ, He will come through for you.

We were crushed and overwhelmed beyond our ability to endure, and we thought we would never live through it. In fact, we expected to die. But as a result, we stopped relying on ourselves and learned to rely only on God, who raises the dead.

2 Corinthians 1:8-9

▶ **Set boundaries:** Define and set healthy boundaries and be assertive about the boundaries. Define your limits, it can be physical, emotional, or even digital. Make it known, communicate it, and remind people, if needed. For example: Ability to prioritise 'ME' or personal time for self-care. What amount can you loan an individual that would not break you? Define boundaries and set the boundaries. Do not be afraid to say 'No.'

▶ **Increase your capacity:** When you think you know, the more you realise and discover that you barely know anything. There is immense potential in you. Keep learning and stretching yourself. I learn every day; I learn from the young and old. Authoring this book, I am enlightened, and I believe you will learn also.

▶ **Take risks:** The Bible, in Hebrews 11:6 says: *Without faith, it is impossible to please God.* Faith is about taking risks. Take big risks and have daring faith. Dream big! Go after your God-given dreams, visions, and purpose. Take challenges, take risks. Take big risks in faith.

▶ **Ask questions:** Ask yourself intriguing, thought-provoking questions. This will help you achieve answers to comprehend you. I ask myself questions such as: How did I get here? Why did I act in a particular way? What could I have done better? You can ask yourself honest questions. Ask for help, favour, haggle, and negotiate prices. There is no harm in asking. If I ask and it is a 'no,' so be it. If you do not ask, you will never know the options or likely answers. Ask curious questions, this can make you understand why things are done in a particular way. 'Why,' answers a lot of questions, hence, so many times, children ask questions, because they want to understand things. By asking, I learn, and I have been able to appreciate and develop myself till date.

▶ **Self-Discovery:** Find out who you are, realise your self-identity. Why do you do what you do? What do you like? What don't you like? What are your strengths and weaknesses?

▶ **Take inventory:** Regular inventory and self-appraisal helps you identify changes to be made and progress already made leading to self-growth and promoting self- awareness. This helps you look inward, take responsibility for your actions and inactions. You need to do this honestly to maximise the benefits.

▶ **Eternity in perspective:** Heaven and hell are real. It is good to have that understanding in view. This is a check, reminding you that you don't want to lose the wonderful sight of your future in Christ. As a believer, having eternity in perspective changes your attitude, motive, and decisions in your everyday life. Just looking around the world today, you can feel hopeless, but with eternity in perspective, you know this life is not all there is. This allows you to focus on things that are eternal and not temporal.

▶ **Try new things:** Learn something new daily. Growing minds and successful people seize the day and opportunities, focus, and eliminate distractions. If you hear an unfamiliar word, and you do not understand it, get a dictionary, or get on the internet and use the search engine to learn the new word. This will increase your vocabulary. Learn new skills – you can learn that skill you have always desired. Do not just leave it in the realm of wishful thinking or dream.

▶ **Be open to change:** Life is all about change, especially, if you are working in the Information Technology (IT) space. Technology is always evolving, and you must stay up to date. It comes with a few challenges – study, and keeping abreast of developments, but the benefits outweigh the challenges. You remain relevant and you discover better and more efficient ways to resolve problems.

▶ **Guard and Renew your mind:** The mind is a battleground; you need to guard what goes into it. I am very careful what I watch, hear, think. What I feed my mind is very important as these produce my action or inaction.

▶ **Delay gratifications:** This is the ability to defer immediate benefits or experience till later. In the process, you produce self-control for later or future well-deserved benefit. True and sustained success requires self-control— delayed gratification. Tony Robbins says, "The ability to hold out now for a better reward later is an essential life skill." This has helped me to be accountable to myself, hindered impulse purchases, and enhanced my self-discipline. This is not to say I do not celebrate little wins; I do, and you should. But delay gratifications for a successful and effective lifestyle.

▶ **Choices:** You are a product of your choice. I am a total summation of several choices I have made. It is important to make informed and God-guided choices in all spheres of life. Let your gut instincts, the Holy Spirit, guide you in all your decision-making. It is okay to make analysis, however, over-analysis can lead to paralysis. Step out and act on your decisions.

"The ability to hold out now for a better reward later is an essential life skill"

Tony Robbins

In conclusion, regardless of where you are in your story, God is able to rewrite it. He can transform your mess into a meaningful message. Never waste any pain, it is part of your story. Embrace your entire story and be willing to share it.

Your story is unique and exclusive; God made you go through it to be a source of inspiration to others. Your deepest pain might be your ministry, your purpose in life. Live out your story to the fullest, recognizing that time is limited. Document your experiences, share your story, and heal the world to make it a better place for you and others.

"Your greatest pain, may be your ministry, purpose in life."

CALL TO ACTION

▶ **Identify Current Difficulties:** Reflect on and list the specific challenges you are facing.

▶ **Rely on Jesus Christ:** Consciously decide to trust Jesus completely with your burdens. Pray and surrender your difficulties to Him.

▶ **Respect Access to Others:** Identify the people to whom you have privileged access and commit to valuing and respecting that access.

▶ **Learn Key Life Lessons:** Identify essential principles or wisdom that can guide you through life. Write them down and reflect on how to apply them.

▶ **Document and Share Your Story:** Think about a significant experience or lesson from your life. Write it down and find a way to share it with others, whether through a blog, social media, or a community group.

Appendix

QUOTES

Chapter 1

1. *"Life is a song; we each get to write our own lyrics."* – **Unknown**

2. *"Life is a puzzle; you can only see the picture when you put all the pieces together."* – **Unknown**

3. *"Your life story is a gift and should be treated as such."* – **Emily V. Gordon**

4. *"The universe is made of stories, not atoms."* – **Muriel Rukeyser.**

5. *"Never underestimate the difference YOU can make in the lives of others."* – **Martin Luther King Jr.**

6. *"We need to know that we make a positive difference through the work we do."* – **Mike Anderson**

7. *"If you can't pay it back, pay it forward."* – **Catherine Ryan Hyde**

8. *"The graveyard is the richest place on the surface of the earth because there you will see the books that were not published, ideas that were not harnessed, songs that were not sung, and drama pieces that were never acted."* – **Myles Munroe**

9. *"The graveyard is the richest place on earth, because it is here that you will find all the hopes and dreams that were never fulfilled, the books that were never written, the songs that were never sung, the inventions that were never shared, the cures that were never discovered, all because someone was too afraid*

to take that first step, keep with the problem, or determined to carry out their dream." – **Les Brown**

10. *"Service to others is the rent you pay for your room here on earth."* – **Muhammad Ali**

11. *"Give, and it will be given to you: good measure, pressed down, shaken together, and running over will be put into your bosom. For with the same measure that you use, it will be measured back to you."* – **Luke 6:38**

12. *"I tell you the truth, unless a kernel of wheat is planted in the soil and dies, it remains alone. But its death will produce many new kernels—a plentiful harvest of new lives."* – **John 12:24**

13. *"Therefore, if anyone is in Christ, he is a new creation; old things have passed away; behold, all things have become new."* – **2 Corinthians 5:17**

14. *"Our stories are powerful especially when they are fuelled with love, compassion, courage, and the strong desire to help those who are just beginning their healing journey. Stories are powerful so please consider sharing your story. Your story, your voice, and your message matters."* – **Treena Wynes**

Chapter 2

1. *"Many stories matter. Stories have been used to dispossess and to malign. But stories can also be used to empower, and to humanise. Stories can break the dignity of a people. But stories can also repair that broken dignity."* – **Chimamanda Ngozi Adichie**

2. *"Whether you know it or not, your desire to write comes from the urge to not just be "creative," it is a need (one every human being on earth has) to help others. A well-told Story*

is a gift to the reader/listener/viewer because it teaches them how to confront their own discomforts." – **Shawn Coyne**

3. "The power of storytelling is undisputed, it's how we connect with people, build movements, and nurture cultures." – **Tyler Kelley**

4. "You saw me before I was born. Every day of my life was recorded in your book. Every moment was laid out before a single day had passed. 17 How precious are your thoughts about me, O God. They cannot be numbered! 18 I cannot even count them; they outnumber the grains of sand! And when I wake up, you are still with me!" – **Psalms 139:16-18**

Chapter 3

1. "Many stories matter. Stories have been used to dispossess and to malign. But stories can also be used to empower, and to humanise. Stories can break the dignity of a people. But stories can also repair that broken dignity." - **Chimamanda Ngozi Adichie**

2. "I'm writing my story so that others might see fragments of themselves." - **Lena Waithe**

3. "Whether you know it or not, your desire to write comes from the urge to not just be "creative," it is a need (one every human being on earth has) to help others. A well-told Story is a gift to the reader/listener/viewer because it teaches them how to confront their own discomforts." - **Shawn Coyne**

4. "Every single time you feel something, if you don't express it, you are robbing the planet of your heart." - **Sheila Kelley**

5. "Your story matters. More importantly, you matter."

6. *"We all have a story. The difference is: do you use the story to empower yourself? Or do you use your story to keep yourself a victim? The question itself empowers you to change your life."* **- Sunny Dawn Johnston**

7. *"Ever read someone's story and think: This is exactly what I needed to hear today! Your story will do that for someone else."*

8. *"Our stories have the power to break down barriers."*

9. *"A picture is worth a thousand words."* **- Unknown**

10. *"The truth is the best picture, the best propaganda."* **- Robert Capa**

11. *"A picture can hide as much as it reveals."* - *Alexandra Petri*

12. *"You're never going to kill storytelling, because it's built in the human plan. We come with it."* **- Margaret Atwood**

13. *"Everybody has their own story; everybody has their own journey."* **Thalia**

14. *"Every story I create, creates me. I write to create myself."* - **Octavia E. Butler**

15. *"To know your future, you must know your past"* - **George Santayana**

16. *"Our future depends on how we understand the past."*- **Gustavo Cerati**

17. *"People must know the past to understand the present, and to face the future"* - **Nellie L McClung**

18. *"Sometimes it takes a painful experience to make us change our ways."*

19. Proverbs 20:30

Chapter 4

1. *"Blessed is the one who considers the poor! In the day of trouble, the Lord delivers him;"* - **Psalm 41:1**

2. *"Whoever despises his neighbour is a sinner, but blessed is he who is generous to the poor."* - **Proverbs 14:21**

3. *"Jesus answered, "Neither this man nor his parents sinned, but it was so that the works of God might be displayed and illustrated in him."* - **John 9:3**

4. *"Don't you remember the rule we had when we lived with you? "If you don't work, you don't eat." And now we are getting reports that a bunch of lazy good-for-nothings are taking advantage of you. This must not be tolerated. We command them to get to work immediately—no excuses, no arguments—and earn their own keep. Friends, do not slack off in doing your duty."* - **2 Thessalonians 3:10-13**

5. *"You are not in a competition with your spouse"* – **Jumoke Akintunde**

6. *"Fight for your marriage, fight for your family."*- **Jumoke Akintunde**

7. *"Sex never keeps a man – keep the bed undefiled, guys zip up, ladies close-up."* – **Jumoke Akintunde**

8. *"Your spouse is not your enemy. The real enemy is the devil."* – **Jumoke Akintunde**

Chapter 5

1. *"Pain has its own noble joy, when it starts a strong consciousness of life, from a stagnant one."* – **John Sterling**

2. *"Pain nourishes courage. You can't be brave if you've only

had wonderful things happen to you." — **Mary Tyler Moore**

3. "You never know how strong you are... until being strong is the only choice you have." — **Cayla Mills**

4. "Pain pays the income of each precious thing." — **William Shakespeare**

5. "Every challenge you face today makes you stronger tomorrow. The challenge of life is intended to make you better, not bitter." — **Roy T. Bennett**

6. "Tough times are inevitable in life and in business. But how you compose yourself during those times defines your spirit and will define your future." — **Richard Branson**

7. "You will have tribulation in this world. Don't be surprised by it, but I speak peace into the middle of that, because I take heart. I have come because I, oh, take heart in this, I have overcome the world." Jesus says. — **John 16:33**

8. "The struggle is part of the story."

9. "Tears are words that need to be written." — **Paulo Coelho**

10. "No pain no glory, turn your pain to gain, your gain is wealth" — **Jumoke Akintunde**

11. "Pain nourishes courage. You can't be brave if you've only had wonderful things happen to you." — **Mary Tyler Moore**

12. "Turn your wounds into wisdom." — **Oprah Winfrey**

13. "Failure gave me strength. Pain was my motivation." — **Michael Jordan**

14. "Pain pays the income of each precious thing." — **William Shakespeare**

15. *"The truth is, we all face hardships of some kind, and you never know the struggles a person is going through. Behind every smile, there's a story of a personal struggle."* — **Adrienne C. Moore**

16. *"Then Jesus said, 'Father, forgive them; for they do not know what they're doing...'"* — **Luke 23:34**

17. *"You never know how strong you are... until being strong is the only choice you have."* — **Cayla Mills**

18. *"Problems can become opportunities when the right people come together."* — **Robert Redford**

19. *"Whenever you see darkness, there is an extraordinary opportunity for the light to burn brighter."* — **Bono**

20. *"Faith is the strength by which a shattered world shall emerge into the light."* — **Helen Keller**

21. *"Finding the lesson behind every adversity will be the one important thing that helps get you through it."* — **Roy T. Bennett**

22. *"We read to know we are not alone."* — **C.S. Lewis**

23. *"I think books are like people, in the sense that they'll turn up in your life when you most need them."* – Emma Thompson

24. *"Life is about accepting the challenges along the way, choosing to keep moving forward and savouring the journey."* — **Roy T. Bennett**

25. *"When things do not go your way, remember that every challenge — every adversity — contains within it the seeds of opportunity and growth."* — **Roy T. Bennett**

26. *"Never run from your pain, acknowledge it and face it"* – **Jumoke Akintunde**

27. *"Leadership is learned daily, not in a day."* - **John Maxwell**

28. *"Leadership can be learned over time, and that willingness and ability to learn is what separates leaders and followers."* - **John Maxwell**

29. *"Then all the congregation raised a loud cry, and the people wept that night. 2 And all the people of Israel grumbled against Moses and Aaron. The whole congregation said to them, "Would that we had died in the land of Egypt! Or would that we had died in this wilderness! 3 Why is the LORD bringing us into this land, to fall by the sword? Our wives and our little ones will become a prey. Would it not be better for us to go back to Egypt?" 4 And they said to one another, "Let us choose a leader and go back to Egypt."* - **Numbers 14:1–4**

30. *"I can guarantee this truth: This is what will be done for someone who doesn't doubt but believes what he says will happen: He can say to this mountain, 'Be uprooted and thrown into the sea,' and it will be done for him."* - **Mark 11:23**

31. *"A person of great understanding is patient, but a short temper is the height of stupidity."* - **Proverbs 14:29**

32. *"We can rejoice, too, when we run into problems and trials, for we know that they help us develop endurance."* - **Romans 5:3**

33. *"We ask this so that you will live the kind of lives that prove you belong to the Lord. Then you will want to please him in every way as you grow in producing every kind of*

good work by this knowledge about God. 11 We ask him tostrengthen you by his glorious might with all the power you need to patiently endure everything with joy."- **Colossians 1:10–11**

34. *"And he went a little further, and fell on his face, and prayed, saying, O my Father, if it be possible, let this cup pass from me: nevertheless, not as I will, but as thou wilt." -* **Matthew 26:39**

Chapter 6

1. *"One bad chapter doesn't mean your story is over."*

2. *"The greater the obstacle, the more glory in overcoming it." –* **Molière**

3. *Obstacles don't have to stop you. If you run into a wall, don't turn around and give up. Figure out how to climb it, go through it, or work around it." –* **Michael Jordan**

4. *"Our very survival depends on our ability to stay awake, to adjust to new ideas, to remain vigilant and to face the challenge of change." –* **Martin Luther King Jr.**

5. *"It's not that I'm so smart, it's just that I stay with problems longer." –* **Albert Einstein**

6. *"Don't be distracted by criticism. Remember-the only taste of success some people have is when they take a bite out of you." –* **Zig Ziglar**

7. *"Worry never accomplishes anything. When you have a problem, it is best to concentrate on the solution to that problem, not the problem itself." –* **Thomas D. Willhite**

8. *"You may encounter many defeats, but you must not be defeated. In fact, it may be necessary to encounter the defeats so you can know who you are, what you can rise from, how*

you can still come out of it." — **Maya Angelou**

9. *"We often suffer, but we are never crushed. Even when we don't know what to do, we never give up. In times of trouble, God is with us, and when we are knocked down, we get up again . . . we know that God raised the Lord Jesus to life. And just as God raised Jesus, he will also raise us to life. Then he will bring us into his presence together." —* **2 Corinthians 4:8-9, 14**

10. *"For our present troubles are small and won't last very long. Yet they produce for us a glory that vastly outweighs them and will last forever!" —* **2 Corinthians 4:17**

11. *"Because I know that the lavish supply of the Spirit of Jesus, the Anointed One, and your intercession for me will bring about my deliverance." —***Philippians 1:19**

12. *"This too shall pass." —* **Edward Fitzgerald's Solomon's Seal/2 Corinthians 4:17**

13. *"You can make your hurts, challenges your history and your wins your story." —* **Jumoke Akintunde**

14. *"Be the change that you wish to see in the world." —* **Mahatma Gandhi**

15. *"Failure is simply the opportunity to begin again, this time more intelligently." —* **Henry Ford**

16. *"It's fine to celebrate success but it is more important to heed the lessons of failure." —* **Bill Gates**

17. *"Success is failure in progress." —* **Albert Einstein**

18. *"I've missed more than 9000 shots in my career. I've lost almost 300 games. 26 times, I've been trusted to take the game winning shot and missed. I've failed over and over and over again in my life. And that is why I succeed." —*

Michael Jordan

19. *"Genius is one percent inspiration, ninety-nine percent perspiration."* – **Thomas Edison**

20. *"There's a better way to do - Find it."* – **Thomas Edison**

21. *"Many of life's failures are people who did not realise how close they were to success when they gave up."* – **Thomas Edison**

22. *"We often miss opportunity because it's dressed in overalls and looks like work."* – **Thomas Edison**

23. *"At least there is hope for a tree: If it is cut down, it will sprout again, and its new shoots will not fail."* – **Job 14:7**

24. *"For I know the plans I have for you," says the LORD. "They are plans for good and not for disaster, to give you a future and a hope."* – **Jeremiah 29:11**

25. *"Thy servant kept his father's sheep, and there came a lion, and a bear, and took a lamb out of the flock: and I went out after him, and smote him, and delivered it out of his mouth: and when he arose against me, I caught him by his beard, and smote him, and slew him."* – **1 Samuel 17:34-35**

26. *"Stop comparing yourself to other people: you are an original. We are all different and it's okay."* – **Joyce Meyer**

27. *"No one can make you feel inferior without your consent."* – **Eleanor Rosevelt**

28. *"For there is hope for a tree, if it be cut down, that it will sprout again, and that its shoots will not cease. Though its root grow old in the earth, and its stump die in the soil, yet at the scent of water it will bud and put out branches like a young plant."* – **Job 14:7-9**

29. *"My own rock was rock among rocks. My father was so poor, (that) poor people called him poor. The day he bought an umbrella, we were rejoicing. For the first 18 years of my life, I had no pair of shoes. That is how things were and then I received Jesus Christ. Then things began to change, look at me today."* – **Pastor E. A. Adeboye**

30. *"I lift up my eyes to the hills-- where does my help come from? My help comes from the LORD…"* – **Psalms 121**

31. *"…because I know that the lavish supply of the Spirit of Jesus, the Anointed One, and your intercession for me will bring about my deliverance."* – **Philippians 1:19**

Chapter 7

1. *"Accept the challenges so that you can feel the exhilaration of victory."* – **George S. Patton**

2. *"Victory is sweetest when you've known defeat."* – **Malcolm Forbes**

3. *"Without a plan, there's no attack. Without attack, no victory."* – **Curtis Armstrong**

4. *"Your victory is right around the corner. Never give up."* – **Nicki Minaj**

5. *"Be ashamed to die until you have won some victory for humanity."* – **Horace Mann**

6. *"Victory has a thousand fathers, but defeat is an orphan."* – **John F. Kennedy**

7. *"The first and greatest victory is to conquer yourself; to be conquered by yourself is of all things most shameful and vile."* – **Plato**

8. *God gives us Victory through Jesus* - **1 Corinthians 15:57**

9. But David said to Saul, "Your servant was tending his father's sheep. When a lion or a bear came and took a sheep from the flock, 35 I went out after it and [a]attacked it and rescued the sheep from its mouth; and when it rose up against me, I grabbed it by its mane and struck it and killed it. 36 Your servant has [b]killed both the lion and the bear; and this uncircumcised Philistine will be like one of them, since he has defied the armies of the living God." - **1 Samuel 17:34-36**

10. "Sometimes it takes a painful experience to make us change our ways." — **Proverbs 20:30**

11. "As an entrepreneur, I get things done by sticking to one rule: Scheduling and organising everything I commit to. It might sound like a no-brainer, but most people fail to do this. If you can get into the rhythm of assigning yourself tasks and calendar appointments, you will never find yourself struggling to remember all the things you already forgot at 3 a.m." — **Dennis Najjar**

12. "There is no one on earth who does what is right all the time and never makes a mistake"- **Ecclesiastes 7:20**

13. "The wicked borrow and never pay back." — **Psalm 37:21**

14. "People who promise things that they never give are like clouds and wind that bring no rain" - **Proverbs 25:14**

15. "Underneath this flabby exterior is an enormous lack of character." — **Oscar Levant**

16. "The difference between a successful person and others is not a lack of strength, not a lack of knowledge, but rather a lack of will." — **Vince Lombardi**

17. "So then faith comes by hearing and hearing by the word of God." — **Romans 10:17**

Chapter 8

1. *"All the peoples of the earth are regarded as nothing. He does as he pleases with the powers of heaven and the peoples of the earth. No one can hold back his hand or say to him: 'What have you done?'"* – **Daniel 4: 35**

2. *"So do not fear, for I am with you; do not be dismayed, for I am your God. I will strengthen you and help you; I will uphold you with my righteous right hand."* – **Isaiah 41:10**

3. The Bible says, *"... If God is for us, who can be against us?"* - **Romans 8:31 NIV**

4. *"If you are tired from carrying heavy burdens, come to me and I will give you rest."* – **Matthew 11:28**

5. *"But do not forget this one thing, dear friends: With the Lord a day is like a thousand years, and a thousand years are like a day. The Lord is not slow in keeping his promise, as some understand slowness. He is patient with you, not wanting anyone to perish, but everyone to come to repentance."* – **2 Peter 3:8–9**

6. *"He has made everything beautiful in its time..."* – **Ecclesiastes 3:11**

7. *"What is impossible with man is possible with God."* – **Luke 18:27**

8. *"But my God shall supply all your needs according to his riches in glory by Christ Jesus."* – **Philippians 4:19**

9. *"... as long as an heir is underage, he is no different from a slave, although he owns the whole estate."* – **Galatians 4:1**

10. *"If you . . . know how to give good gifts to your children, how much more will your heavenly Father give . . . to those*

who ask him." – **Luke 11:13**

11. *"For every beast of the forest is mine, The cattle on a thousand hills. I know every bird of the mountains, and everything that moves in the field is mine. If I were hungry, I would not tell you, for the world is mine, and all it contains."* – **Psalm 50:10-12**

12. *"When you ask, you do not receive, because you ask with wrong motives, that you may spend what you get on your pleasures."* – **James 4:3**

13. *"Ye ask, and receive not, because ye ask amiss, that ye may consume it upon your lusts."* – **James 4:3**

14. *"If I had cherished iniquity in my heart, the Lord would not have listened."* – **Psalm 66:18**

15. *"When you sin, the pay you get is death. But God gives you the gift of eternal life because of what Christ Jesus our Lord has done."* – **Romans 6:23**

16. *"Behold, the LORD's hand is not shortened, that it cannot save; neither his ear heavy, that it cannot hear: But your iniquities have separated between you and your God, and your sins have hid his face from you, that he will not hear. For your hands are defiled with blood, and your fingers with iniquity; your lips have spoken lies, your tongue hath muttered perverseness."* – **Isaiah 59:1–3**

17. *"I confess that we have sinned against you. Yes, even my own family and I have sinned! We have sinned terribly by not obeying the commands, decrees, and regulations that you gave us."* – **Nehemiah 1:6-7**

18. *"I trust the Lord God to save me, and I will wait for him to answer my prayer."* – **Micah 7:7**

19. *"He has made everything beautiful in its time. He has also set eternity in the human heart; yet no one can fathom what God has done from beginning to end."* – **Ecclesiastes 3:11**

20. *"For the vision is yet for an appointed time and it hastens to the end [fulfilment]; it will not deceive or disappoint. Though it tarries, wait [earnestly] for it, because it will surely come; it will not be behindhand on its appointed day."* – **Habakkuk 2:3**

21. *"I am the Lord, and when it is time, I will make these things happen quickly."* – **Isaiah 60:22**

22. *"No one who waits for my help will be disappointed."* – **Isaiah 49:23**

23. *"I wait expectantly, trusting God to help, for he has promised."* – **Psalm 130:5**

24. *"…. faith without works is dead also."* – **James 2:26**

25. *"If people say they have faith, but do nothing, their faith is worth nothing."* – **James 2:14**

26. *"Relax, Daniel, he continued, 'don't be afraid. From the moment you decided to humble yourself to receive understanding, your prayer was heard, and I set out to come to you. But I was waylaid by the angel-prince of the kingdom of Persia.*

27. *And was delayed for a good three weeks. But then Michael, one of the chief angel-princes, intervened to help me. I left him there with the prince of the kingdom of Persia. And now I am here to help you understand what will eventually happen to your people. The vision has to do with what is ahead.'"* – **Daniel 10: 12-14**

28. *"Don't try to get out of anything prematurely. Let it do its*

work, so you become mature and well-developed." – **James 1:4**

29. *"Unless the LORD builds the house, they labor in vain who build it; unless the LORD guards the city, the watchman stays awake in vain. It is vain for you to rise up early, to sit up late, to eat the bread of sorrows; for so He gives His beloved sleep" –* **Psalm 127:1-2**

30. *"I have become as a wonder to many, but You are my strong refuge" -* **Psalm 71:7**

31. *"But by the grace of God I am what I am, and His grace toward me was not in vain; but I labored more abundantly than they all, yet not I, but the grace of God which was with me" –* **1 Corinthians 15:10**

32. *"…because no one succeeds by strength alone." –* **1 Samuel 2:9b**

33. *"…And surely I am with you always, to the very end of the age." –* **Matthew 28:20b**

34. *"He that diggeth a pit shall fall into it; and whoso breaketh an hedge, a serpent shall bite him." –* **Ecclesiastes 10:8**

35. *"Behold, I will do a new thing; now shall it spring forth; shall ye not know it? I will even make a way in the wilderness, and rivers in the desert." –* **Isaiah 43:19**

Chapter 9

1. *"Blessed are those who mourn, for they will be comforted." –* **Matthew 5:4**

2. *"We know that in all things God works for the good of those who love him." –* **Romans 8:28**

3. *"God whispers to us in our pleasures, speaks in our*

*conscience, but shouts in our pain." – **C. S. Lewis***

4. *"Sometimes it takes a painful experience to make us change our ways." – **Proverbs 20:30***

5. *"These little troubles are getting us ready for an eternal glory that will make all our troubles seem like nothing. Things that are seen don't last forever, but things that are not seen are eternal. This is why we keep our minds on the things that cannot be seen." – **2 Corinthians 4:17-18***

6. *"God, grant me the serenity to accept the things I cannot change, the courage to change the things I can, and the wisdom to know the difference." – **Reinhold Niebuhr***

7. *"Yesterday is history, tomorrow is a mystery, today is a gift of God, which is why we call it the present." – **Bill Keane***

8. *"In seeking happiness for others, you will find it in yourself." – **Unknown***

9. *"Life is really simple, but we insist on making it complicated." – **Confucius***

10. *"God, grant me the serenity to accept the things I cannot change, the courage to change the things I can, and the wisdom to know the difference." – **Reinhold Niebuhr***

11. *"We don't want you to be ignorant about those who have died. We don't want you to grieve like other people who have no hope." – **1 Thessalonians 4:13***

12. *"When you go through deep waters, I will be with you. When you go through rivers of difficulty, you will not drown. When you walk through the fire of oppression, you will not be burned up; the flames will not consume you." – **Isaiah 43:2***

13. *"Blessed are those who mourn, for they shall be comforted." – **Matthew 5:4***

14. "... If God is for us, who can be against us?" – **Romans 8:31**

15. "God comforts us in all our troubles so that we can comfort others. When they are troubled, we will be able to give them the same comfort God has given us." – **2 Corinthians 1:4**

16. "You don't get over a loss. You can't go under it; you can't go around it. You've got to go through the grief. And if you're scared to express emotion and refuse to go through it, that's where you get stuck." – **Rick Warren (Pastor Rick's Daily Hope)**

17. "A gossip betrays a confidence, but a trustworthy person keeps a secret." – **Proverbs 11:13**

18. "Every season in life has its purpose and lessons to teach; we must be willing to embrace them and grow." – **Unknown**

19. "I have some questions for you." – **Job 38:3**

20. "I know that you can do anything, and no one can stop you. You asked, 'Who is this that questions my wisdom with such ignorance?' It is I—and I was talking about things I knew nothing about, things far too wonderful for me . . . I take back everything I said, and I sit in dust and ashes to show my repentance." – **Job 42:2-3, 6**

21. "...We were crushed and overwhelmed beyond our ability to endure, and we thought we would never live through it. In fact, we expected to die. But as a result, we stopped relying on ourselves and learned to rely only on God, who raises the dead." – **2 Corinthians 1:8-9**

22. "Let us not become weary in doing good, for at the proper time we will reap a harvest if we do not give up. Therefore, as we have opportunity, let us do good to all people, especially

to those who belong to the family of believers." – **Galatians 6: 9-10**

23. "I will bless you," God says to Abraham, "and you will be a blessing...and all peoples on earth will be blessed through you." – **Genesis 12:2-3**

24. "Many people claim to be loyal, but it is hard to find a trustworthy person." – **Proverbs 20:6**

25. "Trust is the currency of any relationship. Once it's gone, the value diminishes." – **Unknown**

26. "He had compassion for them, because they were harassed and helpless, ..." – **Matthew 9:36**

27. "Do not go about spreading slander among your people." – **Leviticus 19:16**

28. "Whoever slanders their neighbour in secret, I will put to silence;" – **Psalm 101:5**

29. "A wicked person listens to deceitful lips; a liar pays attention to a destructive tongue." – **Proverbs 17:4**

30. "My enemies say of me in malice, "When will he die, and his name perish? When one of them comes to see me, he speaks falsely, while his heart gathers slander; then he goes out and spreads it around. All my enemies whisper together against me; they imagine the worst for me, saying, "A vile disease has afflicted him; he will never get up from the place where he lies." Even my close friend, someone I trusted, one who shared my bread, has turned against me." – **Psalm 41:5-9**

31. Jeremiah's messages weren't accommodated, he said, "I hear many whisperings, "Terror on every side! Denounce him! Let's denounce him!" All my friends are waiting for me to slip,

saying, *"Perhaps he will be deceived; then we will prevail over him and take our revenge on him." – **Jeremiah 20:10***

32. *"Everything that we have—right thinking and right living, a clean slate and a fresh start—comes from God by way of Jesus Christ" – **1 Corinthians 1:30***

33. *"Count it all joy, my brothers, when you meet trials of various kinds," – **James: 1:2***

34. *"Without faith it is impossible to please God." –* **Hebrews 11:6**

35. *"The ability to hold out now for a better reward later is an essential life skill." –* **Tony Robbins**

36. *"People don't care how much you know until they know how much you care" –* **Theodore Roosevelt**

SOURCES

Chapter 1:

1. https://www.verywellmind.com/metaphors-for-life-2330716#:~:text=Some%20examples%20of%20metaphors%20for,put%20all%20the%20pieces%20together.%22

2. https://www.goodreads.com/quotes/884712-the-graveyard-is-the-richest-place-on-earth-because-it

3. https://minimalistquotes.com/myles-munroe-quote-138704/

4. https://www.wow4u.com/53-make-a-difference-quotes/

5. https://treenawynes.ca/your-story-matters/

6. Music: Give to the Lord by Ron Kenoly Integrity Music https://youtu.be/mWycjQp4_Pg?si=w37R8nX1OQDpQ7KE

7. Randall, William L, The Story of My Life: Narrative as Metaphor, The Narrative Complexity of Ordinary Life: Tales from the Coffee Shop, Explorations in Narrative Psychology (New York, 2015; online edn, Oxford Academic, 17 September, 2015), https://doi.org/10.1093/acprof:oso/9780199930432.003.0003, accessed 4 September, 2023.

8. The Bible - The New King James Version (NKJV), Good News Translation (GNT) versions.

Chapter 2:

1. https://slamagency.com/the-power-of-storytelling-4-types-of-stories/
2. https://www.studysmarter.co.uk/explanations/english/creative-story/
3. https://www.pancommunications.com/insights/seven-basic-types-of-stories/
4. The Bible - The New King James Version (NKJV), New Living Translation (NLT), Good News Translation (GNT) versions.

Chapter 3:

1. https://everydaypower.com/pain-quotes/
2. https://www.pathways.health/20-chronic-pain-quotes-that-will-help-you-feel-better/
3. https://www.blurb.com/blog/memoirs-biographies-autobiographies/
4. https://becomeawritertoday.com/famous-memoirs/
5. https://www.lifehack.org/articles/communication/15-best-autobiographies-everyone-should-read-least-once-their-life.html
6. https://zinginstruments.com/songs-that-tell-a-story/
7. https://revstevensherrill.wordpress.com/2021/01/15/hymns-and-their-stories-lesson-one/
8. https://kellymcnelis.com/share-your-story-quotes/
9. https://blog.hubspot.com/marketing/storytelling-quotes

10. The Bible - The New King James Version (NKJV), Good News Translation (GNT) versions.

Chapter 4

1. The Bible - The Message (MSG), Amplified Bible.

Chapter 5:

2. https://www.puckermob.com/entertainment/what-are-the-different-ways-of-sharing-stories/

3. https://www.investopedia.com/financial-edge/1010/top-6-reasons-new-businesses-fail.aspx

4. https://medium.com/@uplift.asia/turn-your-pain-into-power-471c5561f537

5. https://www.samhealth.org/about-samaritan/news-search/2022/11/09/sharing-your-life-stories-can-help-you-and-others

6. https://celadonbooks.com/inspiring-quotes-about-books-and-reading/

7. The Bible - The New King James Version (NKJV), King James Version (KJV), Good News Translation (GNT), God's Word Translation (GW), New Living Translation (NLT), English Standard Version (ESV) versions.

8. The 21 Irrefutable Laws of Leadership - John Maxwell

Chapter 6

1. https://yourstory.com/mystory/top-10-inspirational-success-stories

2. https://www.linkedin.com/pulse/having-right-mindset-can-blueprint-success-life-any-fabio-moioli

3. The Bible – CEV, NLT (New Living Translation), GNT (Good News Translation), New Living Translation (NLT), Contemporary English Version (CEV), The Passion Translation (TPT) versions.

4. https://www.lifehack.org/articles/communication/10-famous-failures-that-will-inspire-you-success.html

5. https://www.thomasedison.org/inventions

6. https://www.thomasedison.org/edison-quotes

7. https://www.21kschool.com/blog/success-stories/

8. https://www.ncbi.nlm.nih.gov/pmc/articles/PMC9328531/

9. Music: https://www.youtube.com/watch?v=DWydssGbUBc

10. https://www.channelstv.com/2022/12/25/my-father-was-so-poor-i-had-no-shoes-for-18-years-adeboye/

Chapter 7

1. The Bible - The New King James Version (NKJV), Good News Translation (GNT)

2. https://www.cnbc.com/2020/01/13/mistakes-rich-and-successful-people-never-make-according-to-self-made-millionaires.html

Chapter 8

1. Music – Lord, You Seem So Far Away—I will Sing by Don Moen https://www.youtube.com/h?v=heNoCXmPV9Y&pp=ygUaTG9yZCwgWW91IFNlZW0gU28gR mFyIEF3YXk%3D

2. The Bible - The New King James Version (NKJV), Good News Translation (GNT), New International Version (NIV), King James Version (KJV), Contemporary English Version (CEV), The Message (MSG), New Living Translation (NLT), AMPC, New Century Version (NCV), New International Reader's Version (NIRV) versions, English Standard Version.

Chapter 9

1. How God Uses Grief to Help You Grow - Pastor Rick's Daily Hope - By Rick Warren — 05/02/2023.

2. What to Do When It Doesn't Make Sense, Is Gossip Destroying Your Relationships? Grief Is a Gift - Pastor Rick's Daily Hope.

3. https://medium.com/swlh/21-of-the-worlds-most-powerful-quotes-updated-for-today-and-tomorrow-6b7634358c2

4. Delayed gratification - Tony Robbins https://www.tonyrobbins.com/achieve-lasting-weight-loss/delayed-gratification/

5. https://www.cruse.org.uk/understanding-grief/grief-experiences/traumatic-loss/traumatic-grief/

6. The Bible - The New King James Version (NKJV), Good News Translation (GNT), New Century Version (NCV), English Standard Version (ESV), Contemporary English Version (CEV), New International Version (NIV), GOD'S WORD Translation (GW), New Living Translation (NLT), The Message (MSG), American Standard Version (ASV) versions.

7. The Battlefield of the Mind - Joyce Meyer

Printed in Great Britain
by Amazon